The Therapist's Encounters
with Revenge and Forgiveness

of related interest

Remorse and Reparation
Edited by Murray Cox
Forensic Focus 7
ISBN 1 85302 452 X pb
ISBN 1 85302 451 1 hb

Between Therapists
The Processing of Transference/Countertransference Material
Arthur Robbins
ISBN 1 85302 832 0

Forensic Psychotherapy
Crime, Psychodynamics and the Offender Patient
Edited by Christopher Cordess and Murray Cox
Forensic Focus 1
ISBN 1 85302 634 4 pb
ISBN 1 85302 240 3 hb

Psychiatric Aspects of Justification, Excuse and Mitigation in Anglo-American Criminal Law
Alec Buchanan
Forensic Focus 17
ISBN 1 85302 797 9

Interpersonal Psychoanalytic Perspectives on Relevance, Dismissal and Self Definition
Arthur Feiner
ISBN 1 85302 864 9

The Therapist's Encounters with Revenge and Forgiveness

Mary Sherrill Durham

Jessica Kingsley Publishers
London and Philadelphia

First published in the United Kingdom in 2000 by
Jessica Kingsley Publishers Ltd,
116 Pentonville Road, London
N1 9JB, England
and
325 Chestnut Street,
Philadelphia PA 19106, USA.

www.jkp.com

Library of Congress Cataloging in Publication Data
Durham, Mary Sherrill, 1924–
    The Therapist's encounters with revenge and forgiveness / Mary Sherrill Durham
      p.   cm.
    Includes bibliographical references and index.
    ISBN 1 85302 815 0 (pbk. : alk. paper)
     1. Forgiveness. 2. Psychotherapy. 3. Revenge. I. Title.
RC489.F67D87 2000
616.89'14--dc21   99--42608
                                          CIP

British Library Cataloguing in Publication Data
Durham, Mary Sherrill
    The Therapist's encounters with revenge and forgiveness
    1. Revenge 2. Forgiveness 3. Therapist and patient
    I. Title
    152.4
    ISBN 1 85302 815 0

Printed and Bound in Great Britain by
Athenaeum Press, Gateshead, Tyne and Wear

Contents

Introduction

Since I embarked upon the exploration of revenge and forgiveness as they are encountered by the psychotherapist in his practice, others with whom I have shared my thoughts on this subject have displayed fairly predictable reactions to the two words: revenge and forgiveness. In conversations with friends, colleagues, librarians and others, the word 'revenge' elicits an almost electric response ('Hey, I could give you some great material!'). When the word 'forgiveness' is mentioned, on the other hand, there is usually one of two reactions. Either eyes begin to glaze over and the subject is changed, signifying that something uncomfortable has been introduced – a *should* – or eyes narrow, suggesting a moment of reflection and thoughtful consideration. The latter response indicates that the topic of forgiveness is gaining new notice in our culture – a phenomenon to which I will refer as 'forgiveness' renaissance'.

One cannot open the newspaper or turn on the news channel on television without being immersed in illustrations of revenge. In Northern Ireland, in Oklahoma City, in elementary schools, in the streets, in the bedroom, revenge is wreaked. Apologies, on the other hand, while not usually front page news, are increasingly frequently brought to our attention: for example, requests for forgiveness regarding slavery in the United States, apartheid in Africa, the atrocities of the Holocaust, and the internment of people of Japanese ancestry in the United States during World War II.

An exploration of vengeance, revenge fantasies and vindictiveness as encountered by the therapist, their psychogenesis and treatment, and the granting or the withholding of forgiveness, as encountered in the therapist's work, are the central themes of this writing. To consider first the topic of revenge, in his practice the therapist will find himself encountering expressions of vengeance in essentially two forms:

1. *Vengeful thinking* concerning the perpetrator: retaliatory wishes which surface in the course of the treatment of the anxious, depressed patient who has been used by the parent in an inappropriate and self-serving manner. I have chosen to characterize this patient as the 'Exploited-Repressive' individual.

2. *Vindictiveness*: a pervasive character trait in the individual who has been
    more openly rejected, manipulated or used, and who presents with a
    personality disorder, most often a narcissistic or borderline personality
    disorder. In discussing this patient, the term 'Vindictive Character' is
    used.

Perspectives on revenge in the literature

The Exploited-Repressive individual and revenge fantasies

In the psychoanalytic literature the seminal thinkers addressed the topic of
revenge in terms of individual rather than societal issues. Freud and Melanie Klein
wrote extensively on revenge, as expressed primarily in the realm of fantasy. In
The Interpretation of Dreams, Freud describes the origin of the term 'the Oedipus
complex,' the quintessential paradigm for revenge fantasies, in stating:

> It may be that we were all destined to direct our first sexual impulses toward
> our mothers, and our first impulses of hatred and violence toward our fathers;
> our dreams convince us that we were. King Oedipus, who slew his father Laius
> and wedded his mother Jocasta, is nothing more or less than a wish fulfilment
> – the fulfilment of the wish of our childhood. (1932, pp.255–256)

Gay (1988) describes *Totem and Taboo* as 'Freud's stirring portrayal of that lethal
fraternal rebellion against patriarchy' (p.333) and notes that in his 1909 paper,
'Family romances,' Freud speaks of the 'motives of revenge and retaliation' in the
child who entertains aggressive, punitive fantasies regarding parents who he feels
have slighted him in some way (p.299).

Klein, confirming the existence of the child's ambivalence and destructive
fantasies regarding his parents, addresses the anguish resulting from the hostile
thoughts, and suggests one of the means of later making reparation, when she
states:

> Our grievances against our parents for having frustrated us, together with the
> feelings of hate and revenge to which these have given rise in us, and again, the
> feelings of guilt and despair arising out of this hate and revenge because we
> have injured the parents whom at the same time we loved – all these, in
> phantasy, we may undo in retrospect (taking away some of the grounds for
> hatred) by playing at the same time the parts of loving parents and loving
> children. (1975, p.312)

The children of whom Freud and Klein wrote were to a certain degree aware of
their negative feelings toward their parents, and were able to express them in the
course of their treatment. Their revenge wishes presumably remained in the realm
of fantasy, and through psychoanalysis they were given the opportunity to share
their concerns (with the masters, no less!) and work through their conflicts.

If they had not been able to communicate their revenge fantasies, or if they had
effectively repressed their resentment toward their parents, who we must assume

were in some ways failing to recognize their needs, these youngsters would likely have fit the description of the Exploited-Repressive individual. They would perhaps have developed symptoms and would likely have functioned below their capacity.

It is often true that the individual who has been exploited does not recognize the source of his discomfort, anxiety and depression until there has been psychiatric intervention. His resentment is awakened during the therapeutic process; only then does he begin to entertain fantasies of revenge against his perpetrator, or exploiter.

In remarkably few works dealing with the neurotic patient will one find the word 'revenge' in the index. For example, in Alice Miller's *The Drama of the Gifted Child* (1994), perhaps the best known presentation of the issues of the exploited child, although there are numerous examples of 'dammed up demands, fears, criticism, or envy break[ing] through for the first time' (p.111), the words 'revenge' or 'retaliation' do not appear in the index. This may be accounted for by the fact that as the patient begins to recognize the role he has played vis-à-vis his parents, many of his expressions of outrage and his wishes to 'show them' simply do not seem to the author/therapist to indicate a thirst for revenge, which to many has a negative connotation. Rather, they are seen as 'just deserts'. As this is a matter of interpretation – of focus on the part of the author   it is hoped that in the present writing a new perspective, an alternative lens in the study of revenge in the Exploited-Repressive individual, will be provided. To consider, for example, an eating disorder or a suicidal gesture as symptomatic of a wish to retaliate against a parent or a spouse may lend a useful direction to the work of the therapy.

The Vindictive Character

The literature concerning characterological vindictiveness is quite another matter. There is no need to look in the index to find words signifying the revenge component in work with the Vindictive Character. Karen Horney, Robert Lane, Marvin Daniels and Harold Searles, for example, who wrote extensively about these difficult patients, use the terms 'arrogant-vindictive' and 'pathological vindictiveness,' and speak of 'an addiction to negativity' in describing those patients whose parents have more openly rejected, manipulated or exploited them, and whose thirst for revenge has led them to act out rather than repress their anger. Rather than seek treatment for their child, their parents have likely resorted to punishment; thus, the individual arrives at the therapist's office pan-angry, bearing grudges. There can be extraordinary tensions and pressures in work with the Vindictive Character, and for this reason the authors devote considerably more space to a discussion of transference and countertransference issues associated with the Vindictive Character than those encountered in work with the Exploited-Repressive patient.

Psychotherapy with the Exploited-Repressive individual and the Vindictive Character: 'Slippery slopes' and potential impasses

The Exploited-Repressive patient, who has not overtly questioned, objected to or even recognized his parents' exploitation of him, is likely to be self-effacing and accommodating with the therapist, while the Vindictive Character will tend to be angry, arrogant and resistant to forming a therapeutic alliance. In work with patients in these two categories the challenges are clearly different, each calling for its own skills and degrees of self-awareness in the therapist.

In work with the Exploited-Repressive patient, a stalemate may occur *if the therapist finds himself dealing with his patient in a way which results in a re-exploitation of the patient.* Many professionals in the mental health field, having explored and dealt with their own issues and dynamics, experience an affinity with the Exploited-Repressive patient, and find it natural, if not compelling, to identify with him. This can have negative consequences, due to the effect of 'intersecting primary vulnerabilities in therapeutic relationships,' a phrase used by Elkind (1992) in describing the dangers of overidentification on the part of the therapist. For this reason, he may indulge in 'fanning the flames of vituperation,' encouraging the patient to endlessly air his grievances – a tendency which results in hours of jeremiads on the part of the patient and 'professional coasting' on the part of the therapist.

Gopnik (1998) writes of his experience on the analytic couch in an article which, though it bears the earmarks of a gentle caricature, is devastating in its vignettes of exploitation on the part of the therapist. The article, the subtitle of which is 'Six years on the couch, and the author's shrink did most of the talking,' describes Gopnik's problems *catching his analyst's attention,* as the latter seemed to be either talking or sleeping. Though he says wittily, 'I could never decide whether to sue for malpractice or fall to my knees in gratitude for such an original healer,' and though he ends on a warm note, the author is clearly engaged in autobiographical revenge concerning a relationship which would presumably have ended in a stalemate if the patient had not terminated by leaving the country. Like R, whose case will be discussed in Chapter 1, the patient did not fully recognize the exploitative nature of the therapist's practices until after a termination, which was based upon circumstantial factors. Gopnik's article casts the profession in a very harsh light; however, it describes well the tendency of the Exploited-Repressive patient to passively collude with any attempt on the part of his therapist to take advantage of his obliging nature.

As seen in the case of L, in Chapter 1, with the Exploited-Repressive patient there is a danger of premature termination due to the impact of *shame* as the patient begins to realize the extent to which he has been used by his parents, without objecting or standing up for himself. A serious impasse in the treatment or a precipitous withdrawal may occur if there is no recognition of the devastating effect of shame in the transference. If the patient assumes that the therapist, like other important individuals in his life, has no use for weakness, the unfortunate result may be a flight into health.

The potential pitfalls in work with the Vindictive Character are quite different. There is little danger of the work becoming stale or interminable; the dangers are those of intolerable frustration on the part of the therapist, or an inability or refusal on the part of the patient to give, forgive or to make concessions. The Vindictive Character is likely to have been openly demeaned, and is acutely conscious of his anger. He has become hardened and cynical, and is enraged at the world at large. He often seeks therapy because a crisis has occurred; perhaps he has been rejected by an important person, or he has lost his job and feels angry and unappreciated. He is resentful and vitriolic. He had not tended to explore his relationships or his reactions; he seeks professional help because his rage is out of control and is interfering with his goals. He wants advice on how to get back on track. He may in fact reject or dismiss the therapist's attempts to engage in an exploration of his dynamics, as he wants a solution. Now.

Quite often, the patient will at some point in the treatment direct his vindictiveness against the therapist, who, finding himself frequently devalued and/or envied, in many ways experiences a threat to his own narcissistic equilibrium. Beleaguered by his patient, struggling with his negative counter-transference, after one too many diatribes regarding his practices or his person, he may long to 'wash his hands of the case'. When this happens he may either act out in anger or agree that he is not the best therapist for the enraged patient, and begin to entertain thoughts of making a referral.

An impasse may occur with the Vindictive Character, unrelated to counter-transference, but rather because of the patient's steadfast refusal to consider altering his vindictive stance. Lane *et al.* (1991) describe this 'addiction to negativity,' which, 'when used as a defense or method of relating to others – can lead to a severe disruption of the psychotherapeutic relationship' (p.407). If the patient feels that in relenting, compromising or forgiving he is branding himself a loser, he will continue to pursue his vindictive path, regardless of the therapist's efforts to effect a change. In addition, the *negative therapeutic reaction* described in Chapter 2 – a special form of resistance to the therapy and the therapist – may render the efforts of the therapist ineffective and preclude progress.

Envy of the therapist can be a major obstacle in the treatment, and is a factor experienced primarily, though not exclusively, in work with the Vindictive Character. De Folch (1991) considers envy 'the most difficult obstacle to progress in the analysis'. According to De Folch:

> In clinical practice, it is the envious reactions – produced when better and more hopeful relations arise, that impede progress and plunge the patient back into repetitive acting out. These patients very often maintain a kind of balance between hope and despair, which they have become accustomed to tolerate, but they are frightened by any clear progress, which would exacerbate their uncontrollable envy. Thus the analysis may stagnate. (p.104)

It cannot be said that either of the two categories of patients described above is invariably more interesting, gratifying or easy to work with than the other. One therapist may find the Exploited-Repressive individual tedious and all too fragile, preferring a lively skirmish with the Vindictive Character. There may in fact be a 'fascination factor,' noted by a colleague whose practice includes forensic psychotherapy in a hospital for the criminally insane. On the other hand, another therapist may derive great satisfaction from observing the changes in the Exploited-Repressive patient's awareness and the growth of his courage and self-respect, while dreading the appearance of the Vindictive Character who arrives in his office saying 'Do something!' Whatever his preferences, however, the clinician will do well to remain alert to the potential paradoxes in the work with each, as *without a certain measure of self-scrutiny on the part of the therapist, the Exploited-Repressive patient may in some ways find himself exploited by his therapist, while the Vindictive Character may experience retaliation on the part of the therapist.*

Forgiveness

A recent surge of publicized interest in the topic of forgiveness is seen not only in requests for forgiveness but also in apologies regarding national and international injustices; and individual statements, often unsolicited, granting forgiveness, and often regarded as inscrutable expressions of largess. Inarguably the most widely publicized apology in American history took place in August 1998, when President Clinton spoke to the nation to apologize for damage incurred by the fact that he had failed to be forthcoming concerning an extramarital affair. 'I have misled the country' became the epitome of triteness. In the flood of interviews following this speech there was an expectable divergence in the public's reaction, some conceding that their president should be forgiven (or the scandal forgotten) and others staunchly refusing to consider the actions as forgivable. Interestingly, the words 'contrition' and 'contrite' were used repeatedly – words seemingly brought out and dusted off for the occasion – *as part of the criticism.* 'He was not contrite enough' was the prevailing sentiment, indicating that the question of the apologizer's sincerity is, to many, more important than the words themselves. The lead editorial in the *Washington Post* two days after Clinton's speech probably best states the public's opinion in its title: 'Mea Not So Culpa.' The public was more incensed by the glib nature of the apology than by the behavior which brought about the apology.

'The Forgiveness Movement,' or 'forgiveness' renaissance,' however we choose to view it, gives pause in our thinking regarding our interpretation of the word 'forgiveness' and our view of forgiveness in the process of psychotherapy, where the question of forgiveness usually arises, if at all, in the latter part of the work, after issues of vengeance have been acknowledged and explored. With the Exploited-Repressive patient, forgiveness has seldom been a matter of previous consideration, as the patient has been unaware of the abusive nature of his relationships and has not thought in terms of blame. The Vindictive Character, on the other hand, has not considered forgiveness because the concept is not within his frame of reference in dealing with the perpetrators of his ills.

When and if the question of forgiveness is introduced, it is often met with a sense of obligation rather than with the flavor of passion experienced in encounters with revenge. When seen as a moral-religious issue, forgiveness is often more unsettling to the patient than are the battles or controversies that gave rise to a thirst for revenge. Optimally, forgiveness may be seen in terms of a harmonious closure in the resolution of a difficult relationship: a closure brought about by a process similar to that of mourning, and one which allows the patient to redirect his energy.

Revenge and forgiveness in child and adolescent psychotherapy

The extent to which the child is able to understand the meaning of the words 'pardon' and 'forgive' depends upon his level of development. Until he has attained the capacity to gradually 'let go' of the excitement, pleasures and pain of revenge, until he is capable of graduating from the 'good guy/bad guy' stage of development, he is probably not capable of understanding the process of forgiveness.

The therapist's encounters with revenge in child and adolescent therapy, on the other hand, are predictably frequent. With one child the source of the vengeance may be quite obscure, while with another it may be all too clear who is the object of retaliation. The Exploited-Repressive child is likely to express his vengeance through disruptive symptoms: eating or sleeping disorders, for example, or elective mutism. Seeing these symptoms, in part, as protests or retaliation against his parents or their practices rather than as free-floating anxieties will often provide a helpful focus in work with children who present with baffling and distressing symptoms. With the openly aggressive child, as well, the source of the anger may seem obscure until one gains information about his background which helps to explain his outrage, but which has been defensively withheld by his parent or caretaker. The example of Ralph, in Chapter 4, illustrates the pathogenesis of a vindictiveness which rendered the child unacceptable in a preschool setting, and which, upon closer examination of his home environment, seemed largely justified. Regardless of the source of the vengeance, a certain measure of involvement on the part of the parents is crucial.

In working with young children, and at times in work with adolescents, the source of the patient's psychopathology and the target of his vengeance are often obscure, as the child is usually unable to communicate his conflicts verbally. When the therapist asks himself 'Who is he trying to get even with? And why?', he may have to engage in a certain amount of detective work in order to discover the source of the child's symptoms or behavior. If he assumes that the child is conscious of his motives and asks 'Why do you rip the bedclothes? Who are you mad at?', the chances are that he will get nowhere. The child may not answer because he does not have the answer. Often, however, he will provide crucial clues to the source of his vengeance in his drawings, or in creating a revealing scenario in a dollhouse. This is not to imply that the therapist assumes a retaliatory motive and proceeds to probe for evidence of revenge; if he is alert, however, he will likely detect a 'bad guy' in the fantasies expressed in the child's play. The child, in fact, may himself wish for an explanation of the behavior which is bringing on punishment and the curtailment of his pleasure! As Marta, as described in Chapter 4, expressed it to her therapist: 'Help me find out why I get so mad at my Mom and Dad!'

The therapist's encounters within the legal system

Whether practicing forensic psychotherapy, serving as an expert witness, finding himself a defendant in a malpractice suit or participating in litigation against managed care, in whatever area of the legal system he finds himself, the therapist will encounter some aspect of revenge. The *forensic psychotherapist* treating the mental offender will likely be dealing with vindictiveness in his patient, and will often be treating someone who is the *object* of society's outrage and vengefulness. The *expert witness* is by definition working in an adversarial situation, in which one party is avenging himself against another; and the therapist faces a serious dilemma if he finds himself expected to serve as both therapist and advocate for his patient. Each of the above aspects of legal activity in the work of psychotherapy has an inherently discomfiting quality; and as many writers have noted, forensic work is not for everyone.

On a more personal level, the potential for *malpractice suits* exemplifies the fact that the therapist may find himself the target of a patient's vengeance. Finally, in the past few years the clinician has found himself in the position of litigant against the intrusions of *managed care*. For many practitioners, this is a position highly incompatible with their professional image. And yet, for the very survival of the values of the profession which they have chosen, therapists have found it necessary to seek restitution for the damage inflicted by the Health Maintenance Organizations. Perhaps we prefer to call it seeking justice; and yet, we must acknowledge, it is also seeking revenge.

Note

For the sake of economy of words, the following inclusive terms are used: (1) The male pronoun is used as an inclusive pronoun. (2) The word 'parent' is often used to include primary caretakers. (3) The word 'psychotherapy' is used to include psychoanalysis and psychoanalytic psychotherapy. (4) The word 'patient' may be used to refer to the individual in treatment whether the therapist be in the medical or in a non-medical profession, though in the latter case the word 'client' is technically more correct.

CHAPTER 1

The Exploited-Repressive Patient

The psychogenesis of the Exploited-Repressive patient and the emergence of revenge wishes in psychotherapy

The Exploited-Repressive individual is perhaps best known in psychiatric literature in Alice Miller's *The Drama of the Gifted Child* (1994) He has been a parent to his parents, accommodating their wishes without regard for his own — in fact, he may not be cognizant of his own needs.

Miller decries this role reversal, or 'parentification,' in stating:

> This child had an amazing ability to perceive and respond – unconsciously, to the need of the mother, or of both parents for him to take on the role that had unconsciously been assigned to him – this role secured 'love' for the child – that is, his parents' exploitation. (p.33)

A 'convenient child,' he has developed symptoms, little aware that his anxiety, depression or disorders of eating or sleep may be indicative of repressed resentments and rage. In the course of therapy, as he becomes aware of the role he has played and the price he has paid for playing this role, he will most likely feel outrage, shame and resentment, and a longing for revenge, even if only in the realm of fantasy. This is the individual who, to use Weiss' term, has held *pathogenic beliefs*, acquired in childhood

> from traumatic experiences with parents. The patient's pathogenic beliefs warn the patient that if he or she attempts to gratify certain impulses or to seek certain developmental goals the patient will risk the disruption of his or her all-important parental ties. It is as a consequence of these beliefs that the patient develops fear, anxiety, guilt, shame, or remorse; institutes repressions; and develops symptoms, inhibitions, and faulty object relations. (1990, p.105)

As a result of this process the individual sees himself as the caretaker of his parents. In fiction we see this occur in a concrete sense in Dickens' *Little Dorrit*, whose 'feckless family dependents are her elders,' whose mother died when she was eight years of age, and who 'from that time onward surrenders her childhood to her father's pathetic need for protection' (Andrews 1994, p.86).

This child's sense of well-being, then, depends upon his willingness and ability to meet his parents' narcissistic demands.

Winnicott, in discussing the consequences of 'not good enough mothering,' states that a failure on the mother's part to meet the infant's gestures, substituting her own needs in her relationship with him, leads to a compliance on the part of the infant which represents the earliest stage of the 'False Self'.

> Through this False Self the infant builds up a false set of relationships, and by means of introjection even attains a show of being real, so that the child may grow to be just like mother, nurse, aunt, brother, or whoever dominates the scene. (Davis and Wallbridge 1981, p.51)

Another way of conceptualizing the False Self is in terms of Helene Deutsch's 'as if' personality. Deutsch describes the individual whose 'whole relationship to life has something about it which is lacking in genuineness and yet outwardly runs along "as if it were complete"' (1942, p.302). The patients described by Deutsch are for the most part persons who have been deprived of tenderness and affection in childhood.

> Without satisfactory object cathexes they have learned an imitativeness as a substitute for genuine relationships. They have typically adopted a completely passive attitude to the environment, with a highly plastic readiness to pick up signals from the outer world and to mold [themselves] and [their] behavior accordingly. (p.304)

There is a striking similarity between the personality portrayals in Miller's, Winnicott's and Deutsch's writings and those described by Jane Phillips, an individual diagnosed as suffering from Multiple Personality Disorder, in her autobiographical work, *The Magic Daughter* (1996). Phillips portrays herself as having an uncanny ability to resemble those persons who influenced her and whom she needed to please. Describing herself as 'a female robot' (p.152) with 'a compulsion to project personalities to suit those around me' (p.145), she states that she 'quickly manufactured persons'. The defenses of this devastating disorder, it would appear, may differ more in degree than in character from those of the Exploited-Repressive patient, who has used the defense of repression rather than dissociation.

Phillips' 'female robot,' Miller's 'gifted child,' Winnicott's 'false self' and Deutsch's 'as-if personality' all to some extent characterize the Exploited-Repressive individual who presents for treatment with low self-esteem, depressive tendencies and a tendency to accommodate to the needs of others, at his own considerable expense. In the process of psychotherapy, it is to be expected that he will become conscious of this role and will begin to 'break with former compliant attitudes, no longer needing to appear good, understanding, tolerant, controlled and, above all, without needs' (Miller 1994, p.41). And with this break there will likely be wishes for revenge against the perpetrators of his depression and feelings of inner emptiness. The questions, then, to be addressed in this chapter are: What is the therapist's reaction to this evolving change in the patient? Is the therapist sensitive to embarrassment on the part of the patient, as the latter reveals his self-annihilating compliance with the expectations of his parents? When the exploited patient begins to perceive the nature of his relationship with the exploiter, is there a temptation on the part of the therapist to take on the role of cheerleader for the patient's emerging tendency to express revenge wishes? Is there a tendency to overidentify with the patient?

The case of L

The work with L illustrates several issues of which the therapist must be aware in the treatment of the Exploited-Repressive individual. Among the questions raised are:

1. When do revenge fantasies become unproductive litanies? When is enough enough? At what point does the therapist's empathy become a tendency to fan the flames of the patient's vituperation?

2. Is there an element of shame in the transference, as the patient discovers that he has been exploited? How does the therapist recognize the disruptive force of shame in the transference?

Background

L's reasons for seeking therapy were 'anxiety and low self-esteem'. For several years she had procrastinated in contacting a therapist, although anxiety attacks of alarming proportions had occasionally made it clear that she needed professional help.

L was five years of age when her family emigrated from Scandinavia. The conflicts experienced by L and her two older brothers are reminiscent of those depicted in Henry Roth's *Call it Sleep* and Willa Cather's *My Antonia*, both of which describe the burdens of children whose parents, displaced persons from Eastern European countries, are extremely dependent upon them. For L, this situation resulted in a harsh superego development at a very early age, with an acute sense of family responsibility and difficulty in attaining autonomy, or freedom from parental bonds.

L remembered little about the move to the United States, when the family left their homeland and relatives to 'make their fortune'. Her father had indeed swiftly proceeded to amass considerable wealth in the manufacture of textiles, while her mother, who had left a promising career in the visual arts, turned to writing fiction, spending a major portion of her days at her desk.

Only their native tongue was spoken in the home. Though she spoke excellent English, L's mother maintained that she felt insecure in dealing with neighbors and business persons, thus insulating herself and relying upon her children to be the conduit for communication with the community. Even as she depended upon her children, however, she was in L's recollection preoccupied and detached, much of her energy being devoted to her prose. Thus the children experienced the 'psychic loss of a physically present parent,' as described by Shabad:

> When we define loss solely in terms of physical loss occurring at a certain time and place, we are not doing justice to the phenomenology of the loss experience. A truly psychoanalytic theory of mourning would not be based only upon the objective reality of loss, but would also encompass the subjective perception and personal experience of loss. Because a sense of loss can be experienced even while another person is physically present, it is useful to distinguish loss as a physically evident fact from loss as a subjectively felt state. (1989, p.104)

Shabad uses the term *traumatic theme* to refer to a chronic pattern of frustrating experiences suffered passively in childhood. 'The traumatic themes of a parent's exploitation of a child for narcissistic purposes, the withholding of love, harsh criticisms, moody silences, and excessive intrusiveness all may induce feelings of psychic loss to a greater or lesser degree' (p.107). Thus L experienced the traumatic themes of being used for her mother's purposes and at the same time being excluded from her mother's closed world.

'My mother called me her "first assistant,"' L recalled, 'and I felt very important. But in that atmosphere my brothers just floundered. My parents didn't seem to notice what they were doing until both of them drifted into truancy and drugs; then they were packed off to boarding school, leaving me the sole bridge between my mother and the rest of the world.' L recalled no parental energy spent in PTA meetings, chauffeuring or social entertaining. The family represented a closed circle without, however, a sense of family unity.

Inevitably, as early as latency L's pathogenic belief was that she was responsible for the family's well-being. This message was relayed in both verbal communications and in concrete ways. Her mother not only refused to deal with the merchants in the community, but also declined to take a driver's test, further insulating herself and increasing her dependency on other family members. When L was old enough to ride her bicycle to the market place, she was given the task of doing the grocery shopping. Her experiences represent an example of 'parentification' as described by Glickauf-Hughes and Mehlman: 'The familial interaction pattern in which children and adolescents are assigned roles and responsibilities normally the province of adults in a given culture, but which parents in a particular family have abdicated' (1995, p.214).

L recalled wistfully longing to be sent to boarding school, which to her represented freedom. 'At first I wondered why my brothers got to go away and I didn't,' she said, 'but I soon caught on. My parents couldn't handle my brothers, and they needed me: the good little girl. Of course I felt special, but it wasn't until I went to college that I realized I'd been their flunky.'

In recalling her preadolescent years L described visits by her mother's sister, Aunt Bertie, a maiden aunt who after retiring from her position as housemother in an orphanage made long visits to L's family during the summer months, offering and her brothers a tantalizing taste of warmth and empathy. L recalled a traumatic incident that took place at the neighborhood swimming pool during one of Aunt Bertie's visits. L walked to the pool daily during the summer holidays, spending hours on the diving boards, hoping to enter some competitive events. On this day, she planned to perfect her back dive from the high board. Standing on the board and mentally planning the motions of the dive, her foot slipped and she fell backward, grazing her shoulder on the edge of the rough hemp of the board. She did not cry out, and when the guard ran to help her out of the water she said 'Thanks, but I'm okay'.

The guard applied medication to her shoulder and offered to call her mother, but L declined the offer and proceeded to dress. 'I guess I didn't know how to handle his words of sympathy,' she recalled. 'But for some reason his kindness made me buckle, and I thought I should call home. It's an indescribable feeling, to fall backwards. The shock was worse than the sting in my shoulder.' As she reached her mother by phone she found herself beginning to cry.

'I think you won't believe what she said when I told her what happened,' L said to her therapist. 'She said, "What were you doing up there on that high board in the first place? You'd better come home. And don't forget, we're almost out of milk. You forgot to get it yesterday."' Since there was no question of asking for a ride, L began to walk home, in a state of quiet hysteria. 'Post-traumatic shakes, I guess you'd call it,' she said. 'Well, about midway through the trek, I looked up and who should be walking toward me but Aunt Bertie! She hugged me right there on the sidewalk, and I thought I would completely fall apart.' Her aunt explained that L's mother had not joined her 'because she was at a tricky point in her writing when you called.'

Though she had been deeply touched by Aunt Bertie's warmth and concern, which contrasted with her mother's dismissive attitude, L did not recall feeling anger toward her mother during this traumatic incident. She remembered only feeling that she had made a nuisance of herself by being careless and getting into trouble, and that she had soon thereafter abandoned her dream of diving competitively.

Even after leaving home for college and comparing her experiences with those of her new friends, L tended to repress her feelings about her parents' expectations, for *without a momentous jolt to the belief system, pathogenic beliefs tend to remain unexamined.* Furthermore, not surprisingly, she continued to be an object of exploitation in the college environment. She lent money indiscriminately to her classmates, who seemed to consider the loans as gifts, and had no intention of repaying her. She became sexually promiscuous and underwent at least one abortion before her senior year, considering herself stupid and asking for no support from her partners.

Psychotherapy

It was not until after graduating from college, becoming employed as an editor, living alone and finding herself entertaining suicidal thoughts that L acknowledged her need for professional help. She called a psychologist, with the introduction: 'I think I may have a number of problems.'

Early in her treatment, L commented, 'In my job, I spend so much time poring over other people's words, it's hard to have someone really listen to my own. It's like starting an autobiography.' In this stimulating new milieu, the object of another's interest, she was soon flooded with memories, describing scenes from her childhood in a most picturesque manner.

As she began to perceive the self-serving patterns of her parents' expectations, coupled with their withholding nature, L became extraordinarily resentful. Unwilling to confront them openly, she began to withdraw, curtailing her customary telephone calls and letters, as well as the hours-long journeys to their home, which she had undertaken for many years. She wrote angry letters but tore them up, fearing their effect upon her parents, whom she had begun to see as quite fragile persons. At the same time, she anticipated retaliation of some nature were she to confront them with their 'breach of parenthood', as she put it.

For many weeks L ruminated obsessively, both alone and in her sessions, about her parents' demands, their insensitivity and their self-centeredness. She expressed indignation about the sacrifices she had made on their behalf – indignation directed in part toward herself, as she saw herself as having been 'a patsy' for many years. She reveled in these bursts of outrage. After some time her therapist, beginning to sense that her 'rantings and railings' were beginning to become repetitive, wondered if the treatment might be approaching a stalemate.

When is enough enough?

In *Analysis Terminable and Interminable* Freud states:

> Experience has taught us that psycho-analytic therapy – is a time-consuming business. Hence, from the very first, attempts have been made to shorten the duration of analyses. Such endeavors required no justification; they could claim to be based on the strongest considerations of reason and expediency. But there was probably still at work in them as well some trace of the impatient

contempt with which the medical science of an earlier day regarded the neuroses as being uncalled-for consequences of invisible injuries. (1937, p.213)

Although there was no question of 'impatient contempt' on the part of L or her therapist, both were aware that her ruminating resentment could take on a life of its own. L, in fact, began to find her vengeful castigations of her parents to be 'quite delicious. Even a little bit addictive. A little blaming calls for more.' This statement indicates L's awareness of the luxuriating quality of resentful reminiscing and its potential for threatening the progress of the work.

Ruminating can indeed be delicious. When the pathogenic nature of the patient's early relationships begins to become apparent, long-repressed hostility and spite may rush forth in a torrent which is alarming, exciting and energizing, and often puzzling. The patient experiences disillusionment, usually deidealization of the parent, and often a sense of mortification at the fact that he has unquestioningly accepted a demeaning and painful role. A most economically worded expression of this reaction was delivered by a patient who had been egregiously exploited by his parents since early childhood. Reflecting upon the longstanding abuse, he shouted: 'Good God! How could I have bought into such a scam?'

The patient's realization that he has 'bought into a scam' inevitably gives rise to a burgeoning anger at and a thirst for revenge on those who have made his life miserable and contributed to his depression and/or his symptoms. With the exploited patient the revenge wishes, as they begin to emerge, are often expressed primarily in fantasy and/or in communication with the therapist. The sessions may begin to contain a litany of vituperation, with the obsessive ruminating described by Betty Joseph as 'chuntering...to mutter, murmur, grumble, find fault, complain' (1989, p.131). Simon and Simon (1990) describe this phase as 'getting stuck in the indignation stage,' writing:

> Your rage consumes you. It consumes time and energy as you stew about your painful past experiences, internally curse the people who hurt you, and plot ways to get even. Your anger calls the shots in your life, making it difficult to concentrate on immediate tasks and problems and taking the joy out of joyful occasions. (p.158)

Philip Roth (1969) offers an amusing parody of the patient 'kvetching' about his parents in his analyst's office. After ninety-three pages of rumination about his mother and father, Portnoy says to Dr Spielvogel:

> Whew! Have I got grievances! Do I harbor hatreds I didn't even know were there! Is it the process, Doctor, or is it what we call 'the material'? All I do is complain, the repugnance seems bottomless, and I'm beginning to wonder if maybe enough isn't enough. I hear myself indulging in the kind of ritualized

bellyaching that is just what gives psychoanalytic patients such a bad name with the general public. (p.93)

Approximately fifty-three thousand words later, Portnoy ends a proud anecdote with a very, very long 'ah', whereupon Roth offers this punch line: "'So,' said Dr. Spielvogel, "Now vee may perhaps to begin. Yes?"' (p.274).

Poland (1996) squarely addresses this issue in saying:

> Over time I have been impressed by the intensity of the reactions long analyses can trigger when mentioned to other colleagues. I have seen usually thoughtful analysts react with an almost reflexing horror when told of an analysis that lasted ten, fifteen, or twenty years. They often took such length to imply at the least stalemate and at the worst exploitation, reacting as if the only real question were whether the practicing analyst were stupid or, instead, a knave. (p.203)

> ...from the dim memory of my early medical training, one basic principle survives across the years. It is that the proper dose of any medicine is *enough*. Enough, and no more. But how much is enough? And enough for whom? If we wonder for an analysis what is long enough, what is too long, when we must ask what it is that we are trying to do. How long a journey should take depends on how far the destination lies. And how is one to decide that? (p.206)

Patients may become so addicted to 'chuntering' that the tendency pervades many areas of their lives. I recall with some amusement a colleague at a mental health center who walked into my office one morning, leaned on my desk and sighed, saying 'I had to walk two miles to the dentist!' I was puzzled, and assumed that his car had broken down on the way to his dental appointment; it was not until he continued his account of this imposition that I realized that he was referring to his parents' abusively indifferent attitude toward his childhood needs. At the age of ten, I learned, he was considered responsible for making and keeping his own dental appointments. Thirty years later, in the early phase of psychoanalysis, my colleague was so consumed with reliving those travesties that he was prone to 'boiling over' in the company of anyone who might listen, without thinking to supply the context of his vignette.

It is not difficult to imagine the content and flavor of my colleague's analytic sessions at this stage in his treatment. This phase is familiar to the therapist who in working with Exploited-Repressive patients has experienced the awakening of resentment, in all of its ragefulness, repetitiveness and perhaps tedium.

The therapist's position

The therapist's position, as the patient's resentment begins to awaken, is suggested by Kirman (1989) in these terms:

In cases of serious depression the analyst must often be careful to allow the revengeful patient to experience fully his right to his feelings ... [However] a too rapid exhortation to verbalize and renounce acting-out may interfere with the cathartic experience or lead the negatively suggestible patient toward action. (p.89)

In order to help the patient to 'experience fully his right to his feelings,' the therapist must recognize that the spiteful feelings are not only legitimate and justified, but that they are also pleasurable and may take on the qualities of a 'high', that is to say, an addiction. In this writer's experience, however, it is not only the 'too rapidly exhorting' therapist who finds himself in a dilemma with the Exploited-Repressive patient who is in the throes of chuntering. The therapist who too rapidly encourages the *catharsis* may in fact find himself *fanning the flames of the patient's vituperation*. If he recognizes that this process is occurring, he will do well to explore his own contribution to the process. It is a heady experience to participate in the opening of a patient's Pandora's box, and it is wise to guard against overzealousness in this venture.

It has been seen that the Exploited-Repressive patient has tended to parent his parents. Therapists, too, may have been subject to exploitation in their own histories. Miller (1994) advises that 'the therapist's sensibility, empathy, responsiveness, and powerful "antennae" indicate that as a child he probably used to fulfill other people's needs and to repress his own' (p.44). Furthermore, as Miller points out, the therapist, if he has not worked through his own resentment toward his parents, may unwittingly live through his exploited patients. When this occurs, the patient, with his own 'powerful antennae,' senses that the therapist *wishes to share his resentment*, and accordingly provides material justifying his rage, in order to please the therapist.

According to this formulation, the patient, obsessively chuntering, becomes a conduit for a supply of satisfaction for the therapist in a process which could theoretically continue ad infinitum: a regrettable situation indeed, as it can be considered, in a sense, to be exploitation on the part of the therapist. When both patient and therapist indulge in repetitive mulling over past indignities and injustices on the part of the parents the therapy may eventually become seriously compromised. Stated in less elegant terms, when the griping takes on a static quality the patient and the therapist may be said to be in *unexamined cahoots*, with the goal of getting even with the exploiters.

The patient may be motivated to continue the chuntering by a wish to please the therapist in this 'collusion against the parents'. If the therapist senses that the content of the sessions may be driven by a transferential motive to please he will be wise to consider his part in a collusion, which will be detrimental to the patient and to the treatment. This potentially destructive situation will be described later in the presentation of the case of R.

Ideally, the patient will be the one to determine when enough chuntering is enough. Most frequently he will begin to sense a repetitive quality in his monologues. If he senses an addictive quality in his communications with his therapist he may begrudge the time and resources spent in castigating his perpetrators. He may realize that he actually remains under his parents' control *so long as he remains focused upon railing against them in his fantasies and in his therapy.* There are many subtle ways, however, in which therapist and patient together affect the direction of the work. The therapist is wise to listen for signs that the patient is inhibiting his expressions of outrage toward the exploiting parents, through fear that he is either becoming tiresome to the therapist or appearing to be shamefully lacking in self-respect. On the other hand, if the therapist finds himself co-chuntering, or indulging in vicarious revenge, or if he is yielding to a temptation to coast, he will prolong the revenge-seeking period of the work, delaying a resolution of the patient's conflicts and a redirection of his energies.

The determination to fail

Coen (in press) discusses the very antithesis of this problem in an article entitled 'How to help patients (and analysts) bear the unbearable: paradoxes in psycho-analytic technique,' in which he addresses the therapist's position in cases where the patient attempts to keep the therapist 'locked into an unsatisfying parent/ child bond in which the couple stays together despite how angry and critical [they] each feel, repeating aspects of the mother/child relationship' (p.26). In a manner which is refreshingly candid, Coen describes his own struggles in situations involving vindictive clinging on the part of two patients who seemed determined to 'derail' his analytic work and who, over extended periods of time, had created considerable discomfort for him. This phenomenon might be con-sidered reverse exploitation, as the patients were creating angst in the therapist by attempting to 'preserve a relationship in which neither person could function alone satisfactorily' and refusing to acknowledge 'the substantial differences between the current analytic relationship and the previous pathological mother/ child relationship' (p.30). This impasse, of course, is more likely to occur in work with the Vindictive Character, to be described in a later chapter, than with the Exploited-Repressive individual; and yet the latter patient, having dealt with some of the issues which brought him to treatment, may 'about face' and direct his revenge wishes toward the therapist in the manner described by Coen. In this situation, of course, there is no doubt about the fact that enough has been enough already; the problem is then one of analyzing the patient's goals.

Shame in the transference: The danger of premature termination

At the height of the period of tirades, L rather abruptly began to introduce new and more neutral issues: practical matters and career concerns. Although these matters were of genuine importance to her, the sessions began to seem flat and lacking in focus. It was not until she met with fresh reminder of her subservient role in the family that her indignation returned in full force. The occasion was her father's birthday celebration, which she had dutifully attended for many years, at the expense of a half day's travel. When during her second year of therapy she surprised her parents by declining the invitation, they expressed disbelief, hurt and outrage. For several hours after this exchange, L found herself extraordinarily anxious and considered capitulating. She did not do so, however, because, as she later acknowledged, *she was afraid that if she did so she would lose her therapist's respect.*

It is not surprising that in the transference L strove to please her therapist. It was not until the above episode occurred, however, that she realized the extent to which she attempted to meet with what she presumed was her therapist's approval. She recognized, indeed, that in shifting the focus of her sessions away from her acrimonious feelings toward her parents she was in fact trying to avoid disapproval on the part of her therapist: disapproval of her 'endless rantings and ravings'. Worse still was her fear that she might become *boring*.

L seemed to have tailored her presentation of material to accede to the presumed interests or needs of her therapist, her 'antennae' apparently seeking out and finding clues in her therapist's responses, which she interpreted as acceptance, indifference or disapproval. Only through a severe emotional jolt – the birthday episode – was she able to discern that once again she had repressed her feelings, suppressing her ambivalence toward her father in order to accommodate the therapist/parent figure.

After exploring the many ramifications of the birthday episode, L found herself with new energy and enthusiasm, and she proceeded to pursue an abandoned interest: that of writing poetry, for which she had a considerable flair. She recognized that she had unconsciously resisted giving free rein to her talents, as she had associated creative writing with the traits of her schizoid mother, who buried herself in her work to the detriment of the family. 'I was my own worst enemy,' she observed, 'shelving my poetry and plugging away at editing. Of course, you don't have to be a hermitress like my mother to be a creative writer.'

Her poetry soon became a passion, providing a new topic which filled her therapy hours, until she became aware that once again she had taken a safer path in order to avoid another painful transferential issue. After some exploration it became clear that L, seemingly having found her niche in resurrecting her writing talents, had been preparing to terminate her therapy, as there remained a sense of discomfort more unsettling than any she had felt during her internal and external struggles with her parents. She had begun to recognize that she was suffering from an extremely anxiety-provoking sense of *shame*: shame not related to her fantasies and expressions of revenge, but shame regarding the fact that for so many years she had been 'witlessly compromising' in her relationship with her parents. *She had come to feel that her therapist could neither like nor respect a person who was such a 'total wimp'; who did not have a mind of her own.*

Reflecting upon the years of exploitation, L did not expect sympathy on the part of her therapist: she feared disdain. Why would any self-respecting person put up with expectations as outlandish as those of her parents? Analyzing the humiliation suffered by L, both historically and in the transference, was perhaps the most difficult aspect of the work. It was fortunate that she did not terminate prematurely, when it might have seemed that all the major issues had been addressed.

Shame, and in particular shame in the transference, is often one of the last elements to be explored in work with the depressed and anxious patient who has lived with exploitation and other kinds of emotional abuse. It may be considered *the dark underside of revenge: shame at having tolerated being the object of abuse.* If not recognized as a potentially powerful motivating factor, transferential shame may lead to a *flight into health.*

The case of R: The 'convenient child' becomes the convenient patient

The vicissitudes of R's psychoanalytic psychotherapy provide an example of a phenomenon which this writer would characterize as 'professional coasting': a tendency on the part of the therapist to settle into a pattern of subtle or not-so-subtle encouragement of expressions of revenge toward the perpetrator of the patient's ills. When such vengeful ideation becomes a focus of the sessions, it can be seen as *a re-exploitation of the exploited patient.*

R sought treatment with Dr B in a state of anxiety, depression and perplexity, following the unanticipated and unheralded termination of five years of psycho-analytic psychotherapy with Dr A. The termination was occasioned by a geographical move on the part of the therapist, who had retired from practice, giving R six weeks' notice of his plan to move to another state. Outlining her predicament, R stated: 'I'm inconsolable. I was devoted to Dr A. When I learned that he was leaving, I was at first shocked, then disillusioned, and now I'm just dismayed. I was on the verge of working through some major issues with my parents, and now I have to start all over again.'

R had not challenged Dr A concerning the abruptness of his announcement of his retirement and relocation. Noting this fact, with its implications of naivety on the part of the patient and a possible lack of forthrightness on the part of the therapist, with some misgivings Dr B agreed to a consultation with R. A certain hesitance about following in the footsteps of Dr A was tempered by the fact that he did not have a personal acquaintance with his departed colleague, nor was he familiar with his work. Therefore he felt that he could have a relatively neutral view of R's predicament. His interest, it should be added, was piqued as R proceeded to describe her background and her experiences as a patient.

Background

R, an elementary school teacher, had begun therapy at the age of forty, motivated by 'a wish to understand myself and be a better person and a better teacher,' and also out of a curiosity about the mysterious process which some of her colleagues discussed in the teachers' lounge. 'I wasn't sure just why I wanted to see a therapist,' she said. 'I was just curious. And before I knew it, I was seeing Dr A three times a week. Well, the amazing part of it was that I didn't realize, until I began describing it, what a strange childhood I'd had, and how self-serving my parents were. I was actually fascinated by my own history! And I found I was an expert in producing little anecdotes about what it was like growing up. I had a treasure trove of memories, most of them rather pathetic. If I'd had seven sessions a week, I still wouldn't have run out of interesting little sketches.'

R's parents were middle-class professionals who lived several hundred miles from R's home at the time of her treatment. She had one sibling, a brother two years younger. She was married, with two children who were in early adolescence at the beginning of her treatment.

R described her childhood family as very closely knit. Her father's teaching profession allowed him freedom during the summer months, during which time the family spent weeks traveling by car. R recalled a six-week journey in a two-door Ford, sitting in the back seat as far from her brother as possible. The children were given a candy bar after dinner if they had not once quarreled during the day.

Early in the work with Dr A, it had become apparent that there were deprivations in R's childhood which she had accepted with a resignation which later astonished her. An example involved her parents' refusal to pay for the 'midmorning snack' at the private girls' school which she attended, on a scholarship. The girls lined up after the third period for juice and crackers: a small dietary supplement which was included in the tuition, but for obscure reasons was not included in the provisions of the scholarship. R's parents considered the snack an indulgence, and chose not to provide for this 'little frill' for R, with the result that she, and only she, did not join her schoolmates for the refreshments. Instead, she retreated alone to the cloakroom to 'study the lockers'.

'I never thought to object,' she recalled. 'I tried not to think about the goodies. My friends pretended it wasn't happening; they probably felt both pity and guilt. And I didn't complain to Mom and Dad, because I had a feeling they didn't really want me in that school anyway, with all those rich girls. If I'd complained, I'd probably have had to listen to a lecture about extravagance.'

Like the above-described patient, L, R developed a sense of obligation toward her parents which continued through her childhood and into adulthood. In her second year of marriage her parents asked her to drive them to a conference several hundred miles from her home. They were 'getting too old to undertake that kind of journey'. R acquiesced, although it meant taking several days' leave from work. Her husband made it clear that he found the request excessive, but it was not until she returned and described the weekend that her parents' exploitation became fully clear to R. 'My husband was just livid,' she said, 'when I told him that when we checked out of the hotel, my father paid for *their* room and handed me the bill for my own.'

R's mother was portrayed as a bitter woman who had been freely indulged as a child, in a family of considerable means. In her marriage, she had expected privileges and prestige in her position as a professor's wife, but found that none of the emoluments of her husband's position were equal to her expectations.

R's relationship with her father was a complicated one. He was stringent in the discipline of the two children, but in private moments R and her father were very close, communicating in a lyrical manner, in a language reserved for the dyad. R shared little confidences with him, telling him what she sensed he wanted to hear. For example, she recalled saying somberly, 'I really don't like Mary Jane. She's too stuck up and spoiled. And she's boy-crazy!' – a statement guaranteed to be met with approval.

R's parents were 'masters at sending conflicting messages'. In *early* adolescence she recalled being invited to take a walk with them; 'as we rounded the first corner they informed me that they expected me to do well in school and later on in college, so that I would be sure to get a good job when I grew up, as *I was not to expect them to support me.* Needless to say, I was blindsided by this pronouncement, made totally out of the blue. I hadn't given that eventuality any thought, as I was about fourteen and had my mind on tomorrow. But I did begin to be convinced of something that I'd somehow known for a long, long time: that I was a burden.'

On this occasion her parents' message thus confirmed an unconscious pathogenic belief concerning R's very presence in her parents' life. At the same time, from a very early age she was given to understand, like L, that her parents depended upon her, in some indiscernible way, for their well-being. This was confirmed when she informed them, at the end of her sophomore year in college, that she planned to drop out, marry and move to another state. Her parents, shocked, expressed a sense of betrayal and abandonment. Truly taken aback, after pondering the news of her 'defection' for several days, they 'called a meeting,' as R phrased it, in which they made it clear that if the marriage should fail, R was not to expect to 'come running home with the children'.

The parental expectations were expressed in yet another and even more confusing a paradigm several years after R's marriage took place, when R's mother made the offhand comment: 'Of course, you recall that *you sold us down the river* by dropping out of school and getting married.' This statement, rich in contradictions, implied that R's parents were her slaves (for who else was 'sold down the river'?) even as she was told, in many ways, that she herself was the runaway slave.

Therapeutic issues: Re-exploitation, 'co-chuntering' and professional coasting

Dr B soon found himself dealing with issues of countertransference regarding R's first therapist, Dr A. He found it necessary to remain cautious about forming opinions concerning the practices of his predecessor, as his only source of information was the word of his distraught new patient. Had Dr A, for example, actually given R only six weeks' notice of his departure, or had she 'not heard' earlier notifications? As Baudry advises:

> A particular window we have on colleagues' style is afforded us by patients who come for a second analysis. I am well aware of the many caveats in such instances, particularly if the first treatment was less than successful. We must take what we hear with several grains of salt, nevertheless; in spite of transference distortions (and I might add, our own competitive wishes!) certain aspects of the previous therapist's style often emerge with surprising clarity. (1991, p.935)

Whatever the facts regarding the termination, its impact was devastating. Dr B's new patient was indeed distressed. 'So many issues were in full tilt when Dr A announced that he was leaving,' she said, 'that I felt like person halfway through a jigsaw puzzle, with the frame all in place and some of the inside pieces lined up – and then someone tilts the table and spills all the parts on the floor.'

The final six weeks of therapy with Dr A had been extraordinarily painful ones for R. 'For five years,' she said, 'he had been my world. He helped me see how outrageous my parents' expectations were. And he helped me free myself from some of their continual demands: like expecting me to write to them once a week, providing what amounted to journals about the kids. I stopped doing that. Now that I think of it, that was kind of mean, getting even like that, but I must say it felt good. Yes, Dr A was my world. He helped me see how spineless I was, and I'm finally learning to tell them off.

'But now I'm beginning to wonder if I wasn't spineless with Dr A, too. Every time I started to bitch about something he expected of me, we ended up talking about *my quirks*. Here's an example: once when he changed his schedule and I objected, *I* was inflexible. This had to do with my afternoons off: Wednesdays. Long after I'd settled into a good routine, seeing him three times a week and keeping Wednesday afternoons sacred, he announced that there would have to be a change in schedule, which meant that the only third weekly hour he had to offer me started at two on Wednesday afternoon. In my own quiet way, I screamed bloody murder. That was *my time!* I was so upset I thought about going to two sessions a week. But then I heard about priorities, as he asked, "What was my therapy for, if not for me?" When I dared to ask why he had to make the change he said it had to do with teaching. How could I presume to compete with the university schedule? And so I lost my afternoon off. That's the way I see it now.'

At this point Dr B found himself troubled by doubts: doubts regarding the necessity of this change. Could it have been in fact that another, more demanding patient had insisted upon seeing Dr A at the hour which was usurped? Or was he squeezing in an interesting new patient while moving his accommodating patient around like a checker on his board?

Now in tears, R protested, 'Every time I started to complain about his giving me so little notice about his moving and leaving me stranded, he managed to turn it around to a conversation about *my neuroses*. How my parents essentially abandoned me when they informed me that they didn't plan to support me after college. He encouraged me to express my feelings about his leaving, but I could tell his heart was already miles away. I could tell, because before I knew it, the subject somehow got changed. I'm sure, now, that he just didn't want to talk about leaving me on such short notice.'

Pondering the patterns in her previous therapy, R continued: 'Now that I think of it, the subject got changed a lot. I've heard the therapist isn't supposed to direct the conversation, but looking back, I believe that all along there were certain things Dr A liked to talk about and things he didn't want to discuss; and I found myself going along with it. Harping away, to please him. Just like with my Dad. I knew what he wanted to hear. I guess you could say I was programmed to be taken advantage of!'

Dr B recalled R's example of tailoring her conversation for her father in complaining that Mary Jane was 'stuck up and boy-crazy.' Would she not also have brought up vignettes about her parents' exploitation, if they seemed to please him, to serve her therapist? She had in fact said in the first session with Dr B that in her previous therapy she would have been able to fill seven sessions a week with 'interesting little sketches' about her childhood.

R herself gradually came to the conclusion that there had been an over-extended period of chuntering in her therapy with Dr A, *in part to oblige the therapist*. Her expressions of resentment toward her parents had begun to take on a static quality – the cycle of spite had begun to take on a life of its own. Whether Dr A had chosen to offer an opportunity for catharsis, or whether he was passively allowing her to remain 'stuck in the indignation state,' upon reflection R began to feel that her relationship with her therapist had been, in some sense, 'a marvelous example of history repeating itself.' Once again she had been accommodating, at her own expense, and once again it was left to her to recognize that in some sense her needs were not being served.

Dr B was familiar with the process of 'co-chuntering', that is, subtly and perhaps unconsciously encouraging the patient's expressions of resentment or fantasies of revenge: *an indulgence at the patient's expense*, and one which can lead to a stalemate. One of his supervisees had commented that 'I know you [Dr B] can spot it a mile away when I'm beginning to wallow in my patient's spite, and egging him on.' Not entirely immune to this tendency himself, Dr B recognized that it is crucial that the therapist himself detect 'professional coasting,' as it prolongs the work, delaying a resolution of the issues which brought the patient to treatment, and, when unchecked, represents a collusion for which he, the therapist, is responsible. Symington (1996) expresses this well when he states 'It is seductive to collude with the patient against a third party' (p.114). He concludes that when there is such a collusion, others in the patient's emotional environment will become 'the baddies' (p.xvi). Poland (1984) addresses this issue in terms of the analyst's neutrality, which, he states, 'involves the analyst's nonself-serving availability as regards who and where the *patient* is' (p.285). He continues with a statement which leaves no doubt as to his feelings about self-serving empathic responses: 'Defensive diffidence is a form of taking sides in the patient's conflicts. To be neutral is not the same as to be neutered' (p.291).

Gabbard and Lester (1996), in a chapter entitled 'Nonsexual boundary violations', discuss *countertransference enactments*, which, 'like the term *projective identification*, imply that the analyst's countertransference is a *joint creation* by patient and analyst' (p.126). In the case of R and Dr A, the therapist's neutrality seems to have been significantly diminished when a countertransference enactment developed, with Dr A colluding with his patient in taking sides against her parents. In this case, however, we must ask, was this collusion a *boundary violation* or a *boundary crossing*? Did Dr A violate neutrality in taking sides, or did he simply prolong the period of castigating R's parents?

Gabbard and Lester respond to this question by asking 'Where is the line between legitimate psychoanalytic work and exploitative boundary violations?', concluding that 'A determination of harm to the patient or the process may assist the analyst in judging the enactment's exploitativeness' (p.127). The fact that the co-chuntering was still in full swing at the time of Dr A's announcement of termination suggests that this was a situation in which there was a serious neutrality–boundary issue, 'in which a repetitive pattern continues without being subject to analytic scrutiny and clearly exploits the patient's vulnerability' (p.130).

It might be said, in fact, that R's revenge wishes, as they emerged in the treatment, were bastardized by the eager support and promotion on the part of her therapist, who seemed indeed to be *coasting professionally*. The sessions with R may have represented to Dr A 'a comfortable hour' in which he did not have to deal with a contentious or critical patient, or with the challenges of a suicidally depressed individual. Perhaps the reader has had the unsettling experience which has befallen this writer, in arriving at sessions with his or her supervisor, prepared to sort out some knotty problems with a recalcitrant patient, only to find in the supervisor a thinly disguised attitude suggesting: 'Ah, now during this hour I can relax. This is a friendly supervisee, not a difficult patient.' The supervisee, depending upon his own ability to recognize and challenge exploitation, may or may not have ways of satisfactorily resolving this situation. The Exploited-Repressive patient, however, by his very nature does not. He is *repressive*; therefore, at least in the early stages of his treatment, he is patently open to *re-exploitation*.

Giving Dr A the benefit of some rather serious doubts concerning neutrality, then, Dr B nevertheless made it clear to R that her complaints demanded respectful consideration. The alternative, of course, was to encourage a repetition of repression of feelings and, worse yet, an apparent dismissal of her new ability to experience and express resentment of the exploitation which she had for so long accepted. Thus for many months Dr B confirmed as quite valid R's bursts of anger concerning her parents and former therapist, and her longing for revenge, while at the same time guarding against becoming a participant in a re-run of R's treatment history by *encouraging* her expressions of outrage: a tendency, he felt, which invariably contributes to a stalemate in the treatment. To quote Symington:

> There is no doubt that a sympathetic listening and an attempt on the part of the psychotherapist to understand the way in which external events have broken the foundations of confidence in the patient are an essential prerequisite of any therapeutic encounter. But is it enough? I think not. If the psychotherapist has not perceived the way in which the patient has actively contributed to his situation, then the patient will feel hopeless. Ultimately, the therapeutic endeavor leaves him as anxious as he was before it started. (1996, p.9)

This raises a question concerning the very aim of the psychotherapeutic process. According to Ticho (1972) a basic analytic technical principle is 'not to become more supportive than is absolutely necessary. This is possible only if the analyst has respect for the patient's dignity, worth, and independence' (p.143). He goes on to say, 'Warmth and kindness without respect for the patient's dignity can lead to smothering and infantilizing the patient' (p.148). In this vein, Symington (1996) asks, 'What is the aim of therapy? Does it aim to make me feel good and whole, or is it to equip me to manage the crises of my life?' (p.177).

The anxiety which had begun to develop during R's sessions with Dr A was felt by Dr B to have been due in part to the fact that she had not recognized the impact of her idealization of her therapist, an idealization which *ipso facto* precluded the development of negative transference responses.

When there are unresolved narcissistic issues on the part of the therapist, the patient's idealization remains unanalyzed. In this situation, according to Finell (1985):

> The analyst is…unable to process or work with the analysand's idealization of him/her, since to do so would be to explore underlying aggression. Aggressive aspects of the transference cannot be processed, since aggression is displaced to 'safe' transferential objects… Since the analysand will not be aware of the tendency to idealize and to feel positively toward the analyst, all the while splitting off and projecting devaluating and hostile feelings to others outside the analytic situation, it is the personal analyst's responsibility to address the problem. (p.434, 435)

It must be assumed that Dr A was aware of the power of R's continuing idealization in the transference, and yet this factor, steadily giving direction to the work, seemed never to have been addressed. Therapists seem to enjoy quoting the saying, 'Don't tamper with the positive transference.' This tongue-in-cheek statement can be translated as 'We're all human' or 'Let me enjoy being God once in a while!'. Though we like to smile about our occasional position on the transference pedestal, it is well to heed the words of McLaughlin (1995) when he states:

> In order for any good to come from what we do, it is necessary that we try to subordinate the primacy of our own needs, that we never presume to know the ground on which we tread or claim right of access to posted fields. (p.435)

McLaughlin later adds, in what I find an unparalleled description of the challenges at the center of this writing: 'As we thread our way through the patients' brambles, we trip over the big feet of our self-interest, then stumble to those same feet to resume the quest for the other' (p.435).

In Dr B's mind, it was of primary importance to be aware of R's 'brambles.' For some time he found R reenacting the patterns of ingratiating herself, flattering her therapist and censoring negative responses. As Dr B pointed out these tendencies,

she was at first exasperated by her own entrenched habits and embarrassed by her
'knee-jerk niceness.'

Some thoughts concerning the follow-up therapist

For Dr B, countertransference issues centered primarily upon the temptation to
assume the role of the good therapist/parent who would provide what his patient
had never adequately experienced: empathy and generosity. He later summed up
his feelings about the work with R in saying: 'This case called for constant
self-examination, representing as it did the kind of challenge that therapists long
for.'

In a collegial discussion concerning the therapist's problems in dealing with
issues involving previous treatment, one participant put it nicely when she said,
'We have no trouble knowing how to deal with the patient who has been abused
by his parents. But it's a truly knotty problem, knowing how to deal with past
therapists' treatment. We have to face our *countertransference to the scenario.*' Ideally,
the therapist will explore the patient's own perceptions of the earlier therapy
relationship without either being confrontational or seeming to blame the
therapist. And yet in countertransference situations it is a rare therapist who does
not at times fall sort of the ideal.

In the light of Dr B's experiences in his work with R, it is interesting to note an
account of the issues confronting the *third therapist,* in the very complicated
situation described by Elkind (1996) in an article entitled 'The impact of negative
experiences as a patient on my work as a therapist.' In this exceptionally candid
article, Elkind, a professional in the practice of psychoanalysis, writes of two
therapy experiences in which her need to be a gratifying patient was not taken
into account, with the result that both therapies ended with negative outcomes.
Fearing that she might precipitate conflicts with her therapists, she only later
realized that she had been regarded as 'an easy, undemanding and satisfied
patient' (p.163). One therapist became arbitrary and unrelenting in his demands,
while the second, who tended to enjoy sharing his own interests with her, did not
seem able to handle the stress of her emotions when she was in crisis. Typically of
the Exploited-Repressive patient, when she became enraged in the transference
and foresaw a dissolution of the relationship she 'regarded this outcome solely as
a reflection of pathology in [herself], not as a dynamic in the relationship or as
related to countertransference' (p.166). This stalemate Elkind considers to be due
to 'intersecting vulnerabilities and defenses of patient and therapist' (p.178),
which to this writer is a most adept description of the mutual frailties in the dyad
when the alliance ends disastrously through, among other factors, professional
coasting and re-exploitation.

Dr Elkind later began treatment with a third analyst, a female, and found the work far more productive. We are not given information about her new analyst's countertransference to the 'previous scenario,' as the patient was not in a position to explore her therapist's feelings about her doubtlessly difficult role. Elkind speculates about the difficulties faced by the analyst only by inference, in saying that she found her to be 'more successful in keeping transference and counter-transference dimensions in focus' (p.168). It would be interesting indeed to know how this experience was perceived by the analyst.

Further vicissitudes of the patient's need to please

The Exploited-Repressive patient, a keen observer of the moods, wishes and preferences of important figures in his life, will be quick to notice and interpret signals sent inadvertently or unconsciously by the therapist. Among the flags that he may interpret subjectively are the following:

1. He may interpret even the most inadvertent sign of impatience on the part of the therapist to signify that his revenge fantasies and wishes are unworthy. A supervisee once related that toward the end of a session with a self-sacrificing, emotionally abused patient, he had glanced toward the clock, only to find his patient in tears. His split-second shift of attention was perceived as indicating restiveness and a devaluation of the patient's accounts of his parents' attitudes. He was astonished to hear the patient say, 'I was waiting for you to say "That's enough out of you" or "Your mother was only trying to do her best" or "At least you had a roof over your head and a coat on your back."' I might add that the therapist had allowed the session to run over his standard limit by ten minutes.

    This is not to imply that the therapist working with the Exploited-Repressive patient should unduly censor his responses, thus inhibiting spontaneity. It is, rather, to suggest that he be alert for signs that for transferential reasons the patient is stifling *his* spontaneity.

2. On the other hand, the patient may be slow to recognize that he is providing material indicting his parents in an effort to comply with the perceived expectations of the therapist. This pattern may occur when the therapist acts as an advocate on his behalf in *a contest against the parents*, in a manner which goes beyond the bounds of neutrality. Objectivity is crucial, and has been rare in the patient's life. It seems likely, in the case of R, that the work with her first therapist, Dr A, had reached a stalemate through 'co-chuntering,' or indulging in ruminative vituperation. When the therapist, for whatever reason, can be perceived as encouraging his patient's expressions of vengefulness against his

exploiters, one consequence is that the content of the therapy sessions becomes focused upon *the perpetrator's pathology* rather than upon *the patient's dynamics* and his reactions to the abuse he has endured. This transgression of neutrality is most likely to occur when the therapist has personal issues similar to those of his patient.

When the therapist thus forms an unacknowledged collusion with the patient, a further danger is that described by Glickhauf-Hughes and Mehlman (1995) in an article on the therapist's narcissism. When therapists 'project their own needs onto clients, thus misperceiving clients' actual dynamics,' they write,

> This can contribute to a problem between therapist and client where therapists subtly discourage clients' negative transference toward them and unconsciously redirect it against 'safe' targets. The therapist is thus less able to help clients work through negative transferences or to process the idealization in the therapeutic relationship. (p.217)

Thus the patient, in his effort to please his therapist, will continue his diatribes against his parents while negative *and positive* transference issues remain unexamined. Strean (1979) discusses the consequences of a failure on the part of the analyst to explore the positive transference, which may represent an unacknowledged or unconscious resistance against negative feelings toward the analyst. Frequently, according to Strean, when the positive transference is not analyzed a second analysis is necessary, as, 'gratified and reinforced [by the first analyst], the negative fantasies and infantile wishes went underground...only to reappear after termination in the form of neuroses and character problems' (p.50).

Strean would in fact seem to be recounting the experience of R in her therapy with Dr A when he states:

> When the patient is psychologically required to suppress and disguise aggressive reactions to frustration, the resistance against feeling and expressing the hateful parts of the love-hate polarity is, of course, maintained, and the unanalyzed positive transference leads to what is really a negative therapeutic reaction after the termination of analysis. (p.501)

As discussed earlier, L's therapy was in danger of being terminated prematurely because of her difficulty in dealing with *shame in the transference*. Like many exploited patients, L had been taught to value strength, independence and duty. At some point in the treatment of the Exploited-Repressive patient, when there is an idealizing transference, there is a danger that the patient will withdraw to some extent out of a fear that he has become a despicably weak victim in the eyes of his therapist. He may fear being asked, 'Why did you put up with that treatment for so long?', implying, 'Where is your self respect?'. His self-esteem, already low, is further damaged if he begins to see himself as 'a total wimp' in the eyes of his therapist.

Thus, when the patient begins to apologize for his acquiescence or make light of the treatment he has endured, the therapist will recognize another aspect of the patient's narcissistic vulnerabilities. When shame is found to affect the direction of the work, stultifying the patient's ability to express freely his hurt and anger, his resentment and his humiliation, it is exceptionally important that the therapist be tactful and empathic, and respectful of the patient's doubts about himself and perhaps his questions about his treatment. Lewis (1981) emphasizes the importance of the recognition of shame in the transference, cautioning that 'unanalyzed shame in the patient–therapist relationship is a particularly potent source of negative therapeutic reactions' (p.249). It will be recalled that L narrowly avoided leaving treatment rather than facing her humiliation vis-à-vis her therapist: her shame at having been so weak in responding to her parents' exploitation. Lewis illuminates this pattern, describing 'a frequent dilemma in shame reactions: they occur in spite of one's better judgment, and compound themselves by making us ashamed that we are ashamed' (p.254).

Lewis offers the following counsel, which I believe will resonate for many of us as we work with the Exploited-Repressive individual:

> Analyzing shame reactions in an atmosphere in which their natural function is taken for granted makes analytic work considerably easier. Pride and shame are, of course, states in which one is aware of an incongruity between the self's 'subjective' reaction and 'objective' circumstances. Ask yourself to explain to yourself or to someone else just what your *ego ideals* are, and unless you are a hopeless prig, you will see how quickly you become ashamed of your ego ideals, i.e., your 'grandiosity'. Because shame and pride involve strong affect, it can seem, for the moment, as if the ego was defective. (pp.261–161)

When the urge for vengeance begins to lose its grip

Begrudging the addiction to revenge fantasies: M's 'folks attacks'

As is true with many Exploited-Repressive patients, R's revenge against her exploiters took place largely in the realm of fantasy. She did 'curtail her services' to her parents to a degree, but she in no major way openly confronted them. However, it was not until she began to consult with Dr B that R recognized that she actually remained under her parents' control *so long as she remained focused upon railing against them in her fantasies and in her therapy.* It was then that she began to see her chuntering as an addiction: a realization which increased her resentment. A further example of frustration with this sense of bondage-by-fantasy addiction is seen in a vignette from the work with M.

A young lawyer who sought therapy because of loneliness, depression and a painful awkwardness in social situations, M soon recognized that he had been exploited by his mother, who had enrolled him in kindergarten at the age of four 'so that she could go back to bed in the morning,' and by his father, who, he said, 'saw me primarily as a star on the football field, although I just wasn't an athletic kid'.

As he began to perceive the sources of his depression, M asked 'Why did it take so long to see that I was being outrageously used? Why didn't I complain?' Complain he did, however, in his sessions, and with increasing gusto. When alone he found himself 'shackled to a compulsion to dream up revenge against my parents. There are what I call "folks attacks"'. In these scenarios M's parents begged forgiveness for all of the abuses perpetrated against him. 'Getting even with the folks,' he explained, somewhat abashed at revealing this gratifying pastime, 'can consume the better part of an evening'.

For a period of time, the fantasies, some of which M shared with his therapist, were a source of great pleasure. Eventually, and gradually, however, his daydreams began to lose their allure; and his therapist recognized that M's vengeance was 'spent' when the latter announced that 'what I need is a Twelve Step Program for people who can't give up bitching about their parents.' He was not, however, simply bitching. His acknowledgement of the gratification obtained through the fantasies and the opportunity to share his thoughts with a non-judgmental therapist allowed M to replace the daydreams with positive action, including setting limits on his parents' demands. 'The "folks attacks" were cluttering up my mind,' he concluded, 'just as the folks managed to clutter up my life'.

Mourning the passing of revenge

In considering that stage in the patient's treatment at which he may be ready to emerge from obsessional revenge fantasies, I turn once again to Joseph and her description of chuntering. Quoting a patient who was attempting to give up chuntering, Joseph (1989) states:

> [The patient] felt that he had almost too much free time on his hands, and had a vague feeling of letdown, or disillusionment as he began to do without them; the sense of letdown coming from the relinquishing of the exciting pain of this dialogue. (p.131)

In spite of this discomfort, which may be experienced as *psychic symptoms of withdrawal*, most patients find that the pleasures of revenge fantasies gradually begin to pale. Eventually it no longer seems worth the energy to dwell upon resentments. This is the state described by Emile Zola in his classic novel, *Germinal*. As Etienne, the young protagonist, walks away from the coal mines where he has spent months of youthful energy in a futile battle against egregious exploitation by the bourgeois Company, he directs his energies toward more constructive and gratifying pursuits. He moves forward. 'His reason,' writes Zola, 'was ripening. He had sown the wild oats of his spite' (1942, p.374).

Even with ripening reason, however, considerable motivation may be required before the Exploited-Repressive individual is able to give up spiteful ruminating. Revenge, as we know, is sweet, and has even been described as *an appetite in itself*. As seen in varying degrees in the cases discussed above, vengeance easily becomes gratifying, even addictive. In the process of relinquishing revenge, the fact that attempts at closure are self-imposed does not make them easier. Even when reason tells him that he has had enough, the individual may ask, 'Why not just a little bit more?'

In order to work through the process of freeing himself from the bondage of vengeance, the patient may need help in *mourning the passing of his revenge wishes*. As Freud stated in *Mourning and Melancholia*, 'Mourning is regularly the reaction to the loss of a loved person, or to *the loss of some abstraction* which has taken the place of one, such as fatherland, liberty, an ideal, and so on' (my italic) (1959, p.153). Unlike the loss of a loved one, the relinquishment of a *gratification* is a matter of choice, and as such is usually made easier when there is some recognition of its difficulty.

The work with L, described above, provides an illustration of some of the issues of loss and mourning in the slow renunciation of obsessive vengefulness. As L proceeded to address a wider range of issues, including her pursuit of creative writing, she occasionally found herself experiencing a sense of loss. 'I miss bitching about my parents,' she might say, with some hesitation. In her freedom to castigate her parents for their manipulations and reversals of roles there had been a delicious sense of 'plucking forbidden fruit.' She occasionally announced, with a mixture of amusement and anxiety: 'I need a fix. I need to gripe a little more about my parents.' Following this overture, she would proceed to relate yet another example of their exploitation: often an incident dating from months or years past. This, in effect, was the flavor of L's period of mourning the passing of her vengeful scorn, and it was complicated, as is generally true of the mourning of a psychic loss, by that feature described by Shabad (1989) as having

> A pernicious, hidden quality…that makes it difficult to grasp, which delays its eventual conscious realization… The incompleteness of psychic loss hinders the adaptive aspects of a mourning process that are typically based upon the finality of the physical loss… Because mourning is so difficult to bring to some closure, psychic loss is continually reexperienced, like salt rubbed into an open wound. (pp.108–109)

Ideally, patient and therapist will recognize more or less simultaneously that stage in the work at which the patient is ready to let go of his addiction to vengefulness and pursue other avenues. As Mrs Hawker expressed it in Angela Huth's story, *Mistral*, 'I'm not one to take offense. It's so time-consuming' (1994, p.88). In obsessively protesting against his parents' treatment of him, the Exploited-

Repressive patient has, of course, taken offense. But if the work goes well, he will, like Mrs Hawker, come to realize that he has *consumed his own time* in vengeful pondering and grudging, and he will proceed to free himself of both his parents' exploitation and his own obsessing by directing his energies in his own chosen direction. In Mitscherlich-Nielsen's words,

> The ability [of an individual] to mourn means that he is able to part with open eyes not only from lost human objects, but also from lost attitudes and thought patterns that governed his life in important periods in his development The work of mourning, a process of leave-taking, is the prerequisite for being able to think new thoughts, perceive new things and alter one's behavior patterns. (1989, p.406)

In mourning the passing of revenge fantasies, the individual has chosen to relinquish a pleasure. This process of course cannot be considered in the same context as that of the loss of a human, personal relationship, as outlined in Horowitz's formulation of the phases of mourning (1989, pp.297–324). In the process of mourning the relinquishment of a gratification, the phases of *outcry* and of *denial* are not included. The phase of *intrusion*, however, is likely to be experienced by the individual who, like M, and L as well, has been inappropriately used, has engaged in revenge fantasies and is attempting to give up the obsessive, resentful ruminating. Optimally, in the working-through process, the individual will feel 'an enhancement of competence' and will be prepared to 'make new commitments to others and to accept new personal roles' (Horowitz 1989, p.297).

Karush (1968) links mourning with the concept of *working through*, which he describes in terms of structural reorganization and overcoming resistances. According to Karush, 'In many ways successful working through repeats a universal developmental process by which energy is provided both for the renunciation of infantile aims and for their replacement by new and more socially acceptable ones' (p.501). Karush's description of the process of working through echoes Freud's (1917) description of mourning as a slow and reluctant submission to the reality principle. Karush emphasizes two ideas in the relationship between mourning and working through: first, working through as mourning for *renounced gratification*, and second, working through as mourning a lost object.

Mourning and creativity

Like L, many patients find avenues of creativity which had been blocked by their addiction to grudges. Pollock (1978) has written extensively on the subject of mourning and its relationship to creativity. As he states,

> In a sense a positive outcome of the mourning or liberation process is creativity – creativity to live happily with oneself and with others, to

creatively participate in various subliminatory pursuits and, in the gifted, to have 'freed energy' to have inspirational ideas and to participate in their elaboration (p.444).

In the context of the present writing, as the power of the grudge is diminished libidinal energy becomes available for investment in new pursuits. Whether or not the individual is, like L, creatively gifted, as he becomes free of the need to ruminate, grouse or entertain schemes of revenge he will enjoy an openness to new relationships and perhaps an enhanced creativity concerning thoughts for his future.

Autobiographical revenge

The compulsion to avenge, as seen in the Exploited-Repressive individual, may be seen in the biography section of even the smallest public library in such works as *Mommy Dearest* by Christina Crawford, the daughter of Joan Crawford; *My Mother's Keeper* by B.D. Hyman, the daughter of Bette Davis; *The Way I See It* by Patti Davis, the daughter of Ronald and Nancy Reagan; and *Going My Way* by Gary Crosby, the son of Bing Crosby. Each of these books tells of egregious exploitation, and in one case, that of Christina Crawford, vicious, persecutory behavior on the part of the parent. With one exception – that of the one male author, Gary Crosby – an early tendency toward denial or repression is depicted in each book, characteristic of the Exploited-Repressive child.

It need not be said that the same stories would not have been seen on the library shelves had they been authored by Jane or John Doe. Thus we cannot escape the conclusion that the authors, with all of their just grievances, in publishing the histories of their parents' insensitive, selfish, exploitative or even cruel treatment were themselves exploiting the names of the stars who had risen to fame. Only one of the authors, Patti Davis, mentions seeking professional help; others made such statements as 'It makes sense to set the record straight,' 'I'm going to make her listen to me. I'm going to write a book' or 'It's a book for all those people who have lived with a terrible secret and have had to hide the truth because they were afraid or because no one would believe them.'

The psychotherapist hears terrible secrets; the patient experiences some relief in unburdening himself or herself of these secrets, and eventually the work goes forward. Neither the therapist nor presumably the patient broadcasts or publishes these secrets, as to do so would mean making the transition from Exploited-Repressive to Vindictive. And this is not the goal of psychotherapy.

CHAPTER 2

The Vindictive Character

Unlike the Exploited-Repressive individual, who is likely to introduce himself to the therapist in a manner indicating a desire to please, the patient whom I have chosen to call the Vindictive Character presents his difficulties with the statement, expressed in one way or another, that he has been crossed or that 'something is not working.' He arrives with a chip on his shoulder. In his view he has been treated unfairly, and his inclination to retaliate is likely to be experienced very soon in the transference.

Early experiences of the Vindictive Character

In *Wild Justice: The Evolution of Revenge*, Jacoby wrote:

> Until the last fifteen years, which have seen a rise of psychiatric interest in narcissistic personality disorders, psychiatrists displayed little interest in analyzing the nature of vindictive aggression. Freud himself had relatively little to say on the specific problem of vindictive drives, although they certainly play a role in a number of the experiences he regarded as critical influences on human development. (1983, p.163)

Horney (1948) and Searles (1965) were among the early writers on the subject of vindictiveness. More extensive research has been undertaken within the past three decades; the writings of Daniels (1967; 1969), Lane (1986; 1995) and Lane, Hull and Foehrenbach (1991) have been found to be most useful as resources regarding the etiology of characterological vindictiveness.

Experiences leading to vindictiveness are manifold, but invariably include a pathological negativity, at some level, directed toward the individual in early years. The negativity may be manifested in the form of outright hostility, physical abuse, or neglect and indifference. In the literature, nowhere have the personality traits and the transference and countertransference issues been more elegantly discussed than in the work of Karen Horney. Horney asks, 'What are the sources of such vindictiveness, and whence its intensity?', answering:

> Like every other neurotic development, this one started in childhood...with particularly bad human experiences and few, if any, redeeming factors. Sheer

brutality, humiliations, derision, neglect, and flagrant hypocrisy, all these assailed a child of especially great sensitivity. [He also] goes through ... a hardening process in order to survive. He may make some pathetic and unsuccessful attempts to win sympathy, interest, or affection but finally chokes off all tender needs. He gradually 'decides' that genuine affection is not only unattainable for him but that it does not exist at all. He ends by no longer wanting it and even rather scorning it. This, however, is a step of grave consequence, because the need for affection, for human warmth and closeness is a powerful incentive for developing qualities that make us likeable. (1950, p.202)

In an article entitled 'The value of vindictiveness' (1948), Horney lists as the three main sources of hostile retaliatory impulses 'Hurt pride, externalization of self-hate, and 'Lebensneid', or the patient's hopelessness about his life' (p.7).

Searles (1965) broadens the spectrum of the etiology of the Vindictive Character in emphasizing the 'important defensive functions' of revenge. He describes it as 'a defense against the awareness of anxiety-laden, repressed emotions – particularly with regard to repressed grief and separation-anxiety – two affects which have been given little cognizance as being among the basic determinants of chronic vindictiveness' (p.177).

In this connection, Socarides (1977) states:

The conscious aim of vengeance is retribution, punishment, and a longed-for state of peace. One finds routinely, however, that the act itself is highly overdetermined. Unconsciously, the aim of the vengeful individual is to hide a more disastrous damage to the ego, a damage experienced during the earliest years of life and underlying the specific injuries of which he complains. In this sense the act of revenge is a defense mechanism whose function is to conceal the deepest traumata of childhood. In psychoanalytic therapy, once the revenge motif is worked through, these primitive conflicts are revealed. (p.407)

Daniels (1969), in considering 'the seeds of pathological vindictiveness,' includes 'repeated instances of disappearing love, [with] forceful grabbing as a major mode of relating to the world,' stemming from 'germinal experiences of disappointment ...accompanied, in time, by the woeful cynicism which characterizes pathological vindictiveness' (p.183). The vindictive character's parents, according to Daniels, 'with their consistent emotional aloofness, flagrant manipulativeness, and behavioral allegiance to the abstractions of justice and requital, thereby foster stabilization of the structural aspects of vindictive thinking' (p.194).

Kohut (1972) sees vindictiveness in terms of a response to narcissistic injury. He states:

The need for revenge, for righting a wrong, for undoing a hurt by whatever means, and a deeply anchored, unrelenting compulsion in the pursuit of all these aims which gives no rest to those who have suffered a narcissistic injury – these are features which are characteristic for the phenomenon of narcissistic rage in all its forms and which set it apart from other kinds of aggression. (p.380)

Daniels (1967) introduces the concept of the 'architectonics' of vindictive thinking: 'the implicit presuppositions upon which such thinking rests.' This concept is related to that of 'pathogenic beliefs,' discussed in relation to the Exploited-Repressive patient, the difference being that Daniels' 'architectonics' are more in the nature of implicit suppositions leading to unwritten but highly reinforced rules laid down by the parents: 'abstract principles of justice' (p.823).

To illustrate, a client, whose reason for referral was 'Depressed: Something went wrong in the second marriage,' related an incident from his childhood in which he returned from school somewhat bruised physically and emotionally after a playground episode in which a classmate had pushed him onto the hardtop in a dispute over who was 'the smartest kid in the class.' When his mother asked, 'Well, what did you do then?', he replied, 'I told the teacher.' His mother, in response, clutched her forehead, saying, 'Well! Just don't tell your father. He would tell you about all the times that very thing happened to *him* on *his* playground and how *he* knocked the kid's block off.' Here, of course, is vindictive thinking in the making. The patient was being taught the architechtonics of the talionic principle, with some added embellishments: 'Sissies tell the teacher – and you're lucky you told me and not your father.' Hearing this vignette, the therapist might anticipate examples of retaliatory behavior on the part of the patient in his two failed marriages.

This client, in fact, proved to be dismissive of his therapist, splenetic in his attitude toward the process of psychotherapy and contentious about limits set by the therapist. Bullied by his father and ridiculed by his mother, he personified many of the characteristics of the Vindictive Character as portrayed by Socarides (1977) when he states:

> Surface manifestations of vengeance achieve almost a classic, unvarying pattern. The person is grudging, unforgiving, remorseless, ruthless, heartless, implacable, and inflexible. He lives for revenge with a single-mindedness of purpose. Passionately he moves toward punitive or retaliatory action. Above all other desires is the one to 'get even' (in effect, to get more than 'even'). Whether he feels and acts from the conviction that he is engaged in 'just retribution' or 'malicious retaliation', the clinical picture is identical. (p.405)

Considering the adjectives in the above quotations, one might wonder why a therapist would consider becoming involved with an individual who fits the nomenclature of the Vindictive Character. And yet, the challenges are met. And we may be sure that the harsh descriptions were born of clinical experience, and that there were rewards in sufficient number to bring the therapists to share their work, with its challenges, its exasperations and its gratifications.

The case of B

The case of B exemplifies many of the defenses and characteristics of the Vindictive Character, including devaluation, jealousy and envy, the negative therapeutic reaction, projective identification and splitting.

A divorcee in her late forties, B sought therapy when she was informed by one of the tenants in the apartment of which she was landlady that she was 'impossible to deal with' and that no one would want to rent from her if she did not change her ways. She was puzzled by 'the tenant uprising,' as she described it, as she felt that she had dealt fairly with the persons to whom she rented. But after 'some unpleasantness' regarding her attitude toward certain children and pets in the apartments, she had received a notice, signed by representatives of her five apartments, stating that there were plenty of other nice dwellings in town to which they would be happy to move if she continued to dismiss their complaints. 'They weren't at all clear about what my obnoxious ways are,' she said, 'but they recommended that I think about it.' She had found it fruitless to think about herself as 'impossible,' and she did not wish to face an upheaval in her life; and so she contacted a psychotherapist for help with this problem.

In a short time, the therapist was given ample evidence of 'the obnoxious ways,' beginning with an unpleasant haughtiness and a sarcastic or dismissive response to any attempt on the therapist's part to gain information. When B finally became resigned to the process of clinical history-taking, she said, 'All right, probe away,' and offered the following information.

Background

B was the only child of parents whom she described as 'socially ambitious and sort of aloof.' Neither her mother nor her father had time to spend with her; her mother always seemed to be brooding about a tragedy which had befallen the family before B was born. In the fifth month of her mother's pregnancy with B, a daughter had died of scarlet fever at the age of five: an inconsolable loss for both parents. They gave B the name of the deceased daughter, thus bestowing upon her, before her birth, the position of 'the replacement child.' Named Belle, B thought of herself as 'Belle Two,' living in the shadow of 'Belle One.'

In many ways B's mother made it clear that B would never measure up to her 'dear departed sister,' who had been a beautiful, warm and loving child. Any expression of hostility on B's part was met with the statement: 'Your sister wouldn't have acted like that.' Not surprisingly, these comments soon fostered a massive grudge toward a sister whom B knew only through comparative illustrations and a host of memorabilia, including photographs of a pretty child wearing a tutu. Among other attributes, Belle One, at the age of five, had been a promising ballet dancer.

B's father, equally devastated by the death of Belle One, made it known that he had hoped that Belle Two would be a boy. 'No one of course could measure up to my sister,' said B, 'so better I'd have been a male child': a poignant statement of the legacy of a small child struggling for a place of worth in her world. B's earliest memories involved efforts to provide some pleasure for her mother, whose grief over Belle One's death seemed all-encompassing. While she was still at nursery school B learned to read, or perhaps to memorize, some of the tales of Beatrix Potter, in the hope of pleasing her mother by reading to her. Her efforts, however, were rebuffed. When her mother referred to Peter Rabbit as 'that silly bunny,' B gave up and began to 'brood in earnest' over ways in which she could *get even with* the sister whom she could not replace.

Thus it was in a politely malevolent environment that B struggled with her hatred toward a dead sibling to whom she could not express her resentment and envy. At an early age she decided that the one way in which she could win some recognition was in becoming 'an even better dancer than Belle One.' She recalled her mother's attitude toward her request for ballet lessons: 'Do I have to go through this again?' she had asked with a sigh. 'This will only bring back memories.' B, however, prevailed upon her mother to provide lessons, and soon discovered that, like her rival, she had considerable talent. Thus, spurred by unrelenting determination and self-discipline, B eventually achieved recognition as an eminently successful prima ballerina. She recalled her years upon the stage as 'the happy period in my life. My parents were sometimes in the audience.' A number of years before becoming the controversial landlady, this period of glory faded to a sorrowful close, as she was forced to recognize that she was no longer able to perform with the dexterity which had earned her 'my place in the sun,' and she retired, reluctantly, from the stage. Her marriage had from the beginning been an unhappy one, and there were no children.

Devaluation

After receiving the ultimatum from her tenants, B contacted a mental health center, saying that she would like to consult with 'someone who is good. But I can't afford the astronomical fees that some people are charging.' Thus setting the tone, she somewhat reluctantly accepted an assignment with one of the senior female therapists, Dr C, who set her fee according to the clinic's sliding scale.

From the beginning of the therapy relationship, B tended, without reservation, to make assessments of the therapist's skills, often asking why she was assigned to

Dr C, or wondering why the therapist's credentials were not framed and displayed on the walls of the office – an office shared by many mental health professionals. She graded the therapist's comments or interpretations according to her own standards of effectiveness, using the word 'clever' to signify approval. She professed never to contemplate, between sessions, what had taken place during the previous meeting. She 'wondered' why the therapist was working for a not-for-profit agency when she might have been making 'real money' in private practice. She brushed aside occasional indications of improvement in her relationship with her tenants, saying that perhaps they were feeling sorry for her, but that for all of Dr C's efforts, she, B, was not gaining any new negotiating skills. Perhaps most destructive to the work was the fact that, unbeknownst to her therapist for many months, B had made the acquaintance of a congenial patient in the waiting room: a woman whose dynamics in many ways resembled those of B, and with whom B graded complaints about their ineffective therapists and the mental health profession in general. These 'sessions' took place immediately preceding B's appointed hour, and added to the content of her sessions vindictive material which B alone might have overlooked.

After two years of escalating devaluation, Dr C found herself feeling grateful that she was not seeing B in her private office. Among other reasons, she became aware of the fact that as the sessions drew to a close, she looked forward to joining her colleagues in the staff lounge where she could vent her exasperation with the woman who had left after one more lengthy period of belittling her efforts.

B had been in treatment for two years, in a relationship which continued in an atmosphere of tenuousness, replete with such statements as 'I'm not sure you're the right therapist for me,' when it was necessary for Dr C abruptly to cancel all appointments for an indeterminate length of time because of a family emergency. The therapist's daughter, traveling in a distant state, had been seriously injured in an automobile accident. Aware of B's distaste for ambiguity, Dr C informed her of the nature of the emergency cancellations. B's response was: 'I'm sorry. I'll try to get along without you.'

Upon Dr C's return, B referred to the interruption with the statement: 'When you called to cancel our meetings, you rather summarily dismissed me.' This rebuke was followed by some enactments of B's narcissistic rage, which had become magnified during Dr C's absence, despite her offhand remark upon learning of the sudden cancellations. She began frequently to cancel appointments, saying that she would actually prefer not to have to make appointments at all, but rather to have an 'open-ended' arrangement.

Jealousy and envy

The crisis of the therapist's emergency, painful for both Dr C and for B, illuminated issues central to the work with B and many vindictive patients: issues of jealousy and envy. The therapist's abrupt announcement that it was necessary to cancel appointments in order to care for *a daughter in crisis* was more than could be tolerated by B, who from her earliest memories had 'played second fiddle' to a sister whom she had never known, and who had suffered, and forever remained first in her parents' affections. Now, confronted with a crisis signifying that a daughter, somewhere out west, was more needy, more important and more worthy of concern than she, her jealousy was agonizing.

B's rage at her 'sister' was intense, but was perhaps secondary to her simmering resentment of the therapist herself, for whom she harbored intense envy. Dr C had credentials which were beyond B's reach; and what's more, as B determined, she *probably did not have to make a living.* Why else, B reasoned, would she be working in a not for profit organization?

If the therapist's emergency had occurred in the very early stages of the work with B, the relationship would probably not have survived, so intense were B's grudging jealousy and envy and so little did it approximate a therapeutic alliance. Jealousy, directed at a rival, can be a significantly disruptive factor in a relationship. The destructive power of envy, however, in work with the Vindictive Character cannot be overemphasized. B's envy of her therapist would seem to fit the description of Shengold's *malignant envy*, which 'descriptively and clinically involves feeling specifically that what the envied other has or is has been robbed from the self,' making it 'a formidable resistance to treatment' (1994, p.182). Klein adds that:

> The envious patient grudges the analyst the success of his work; and if he feels that the analyst and the help he is giving have become spoilt and devalued by his envious criticism, he cannot introject him sufficiently as a good object nor accept his interpretations with real conviction and assimilate them. (1975, p.184)

In an article by Lane on the 'negative supervisory reaction' (1986), many of the manifestations of envy in the supervisee are pertinent to those in the work with B. Lane describes the supervisee who, like the patient with a severe narcissistic character structure, exhibits strong envy and competitiveness with the supervisor, resulting in a failure to develop a dependent transference, 'in order to defend against disappointment, exposure, vulnerability and engulfment' (p.67). B tended to be sparing – indeed, parsimonious – in offering intimations of progress in her treatment, as progress was seen as *a triumph for the therapist.*

In *Billy Budd*, Melville elegantly depicted the destructive nature of envy when he wrote: 'Is Envy then such a monster? Well, though many an arraigned mortal has in hopes of mitigated penalty pleaded guilty to horrible actions, did ever anybody seriously confess to envy? Something there is in it universally felt to be more shameful than even felonious crime' (1969, p.39).

It will be noted that each of the above writers is addressing the damage inflicted upon the envying party rather than upon the envied one. It is this very feature of the relationship which makes envy more insidious than many other emotional states. For reasons of pride, among others, as Melville points out, envy is often inexpressible and thus remains covert and unresolved. Both parties are therefore in disarray, as the envier is in his own private torment, while the envied individual is not privy to the nature of his own apparent offense and is left in a state of consternation. In the relationship between B and Dr C, expressions of envy were relatively explicit, due in part to B's critical waiting-room conversations, which often inflamed her prior to her sessions. Thus, discomfiting as were the envy-based, devaluing attacks, they were out in the open, to be dealt with.

The negative therapeutic reaction

The negative therapeutic reaction, which may be considered a special form of resistance, manifested when the patient becomes engaged in interactions with the therapist which render the therapist ineffective, often results in a worsening of symptoms. The negative reaction to the therapist's interventions may be brought about by envy, competitiveness, masochistic tendencies, a feeling of being hurt or humiliated, or resentment of the fact that in the patient's eyes the therapist has proven himself superior by making an interpretation that 'hits the mark' or even by commenting on progress in the treatment. As Gabbard (1989) states, 'The systematic defeating of treaters through the hateful rejection of their help has a symbolic meaning of revenge against the patient's parents. The patient derives enormous gratification from this fantasy of paying back the parents for their perceived neglect and abuse' (p.102).

The negative therapeutic reaction was a major ingredient in B's therapy, as she tended to resist any indications that her treatment was having a salutary effect. Her envy of Dr C made it difficult for her to acknowledge that progress was being made, and her competitiveness contributed to her belittling of Dr C's approach.

Throughout the period following the emergency interruption in the therapy with B, there were exacerbations of a negative therapeutic reaction, expressed in increasingly provocative devaluation and representing 'a wish,' as described by Lane, 'to retaliate by humiliating the analyst, rendering him ineffective and impotent, thus regaining…supremacy' (1986, p.66).

Projective identification

The work with B serves well to illustrate the phenomenon of projective identification in therapy with the Vindictive Character. This process, in which the therapist finds himself feeling uneasy through a feeling of *being coerced,* is one of the most ubiquitous and also one of the most disquieting aspects of working with this patient. Not surprisingly, Dr C often felt quite uncomfortably under interpersonal pressure to *do something* in order to measure up to B's expectations of a good therapist. There was often the uneasy feeling that she was missing something, that there was a key which another therapist would surely have discovered, but which remained unavailable to her: a key which would have rendered her more 'clever' in the eyes of B. Thus Dr C found herself being somewhat less spontaneous in her exchanges with B than with many of her other patients.

It was not until her daughter's automobile accident and the traumatic interruption that Dr C became aware of the fact that she, the therapist, was in the position of being the recipient of B's disowned feelings of being second-rate. B, as noted, seemed to show little reaction to the sudden cancellations beyond annoyance at being 'summarily dismissed.' In her own distress and shock, Dr C did not at the time of the crisis contemplate the fact that once again a tragedy befalling a 'sibling' was in fact igniting B's angry rivalry. B felt simply 'shoved aside' and not worth much consideration, and through projective identification Dr C had the uneasy sense of being *herself* inadequate.

Upon returning to her office and informing B that her daughter was out of danger and that the work could resume according to schedule, Dr C was dismayed to be told, 'I'm glad. But I thought I should tell you, I talked to several people about your problem with your daughter, and nearly everyone said you shouldn't have given me the details of your personal problems. That was burdening me with something that's none of my business.'

Under most circumstances, B's statement would have been undeniably accurate. As she did not think in terms of exceptions to the rule, her feeling of being once again diminished led her to exact revenge upon the therapist in her own uniquely acerbic manner. And Dr C, pondering this fresh critique of her skills, found herself *feeling somehow chagrined and unprofessional.* She envisioned B canvassing the community, grading her on her professionalism or the lack thereof. She felt inept, inferior, mediocre. Another therapist, she considered, would not have put B in such a position by informing her of her own troubles.

It was not until she had gained some distance from this situation that Dr C realized that she was the recipient of B's despised feelings of inferiority, projected onto her at a moment of injured pride, and at a moment when she was herself decidedly vulnerable. The coercive aspects of B's projection were later clear to Dr

C. And I would suggest that the word 'later' represents a key and characteristic component in this process. The process itself is subtle and unsettling, and is effective 'to the extent that the projection can make contact with existing identity fragments within the recipient' (Knapp 1989, p.56). The therapist was sufficiently introspective to have had moments of doubt about her efficacy, and B had targeted her vulnerabilities with laser-like accuracy.

Splitting

As a replacement child calling herself 'Belle Two', B had been consistently devalued while her parents held up the deceased 'Belle One' as the ideal daughter. In repeating this history, B found every opportunity to express her low opinion of Dr C. In this sense, B's attitude toward her therapist illustrated the defense of splitting, as she came to see Dr C as 'all bad.' Any redeeming features were discounted, as B's experience had taught her that she needed to maintain a negative and wary attitude toward her therapist. At some level B seemed to have argued: 'If I should come to see Dr C as caring and trustworthy, and if I should allow myself to depend upon her, what's to keep my therapist from later becoming my adversary, and in fact abandoning me, just as my parents, my former husband and my tenants have done?' Having experienced psychic abandonment on the part of important people upon whom she had depended, when her therapist unexpectedly gave her 'low priority,' B thus braced herself by declaring: 'I don't need her. She's no good.'

The case of W

W was a young man in his twenties when he sought help, in a state of turmoil after having been discharged from military service because of an obsessive-compulsive disorder. Enraged at the Army and at society in general, he was described in a psychiatric evaluation as 'perfectionistic, sometimes uncontrollably angry. "Has it in" for many tormenters in his past. Worries a great deal, ruminates, has flights of ideas, leads a completely isolated life.'

In his initial therapy sessions W's principal affect was vindictive rage, directed largely toward the 'tormenters in his past,' including government agencies and uncaring school officials. For many weeks the therapist learned little about his more personal relationships, as only sketchy information was offered about even the most important figures in W's life. Gradually, however, he began to be able to allow the therapist to enter into his orbit. After one year of once-weekly sessions, the maximum contact tolerable for him, he announced that it helped to talk to 'someone.' 'But,' he added, 'the benefits last about a half-hour. It's like washing your hair. Very soon it gets greasy again.' With this cautious appraisal of the therapeutic process, he began to contemplate an ongoing relationship.

Thus, after several months of weekly sessions, W proceeded to describe some of the events and relationships of his early years, initially somewhat astonished that someone should be interested in hearing about his childhood. It was therefore with little affect that he began a session, early in the sixth month of treatment, by saying that a family neighbor had recently told him that when he was a toddler she had called Child Protective Services to report that his mother made a practice of sending him out into the back yard, locking the door and leaving him alone and unsupervised for hours at a time. At that point in his treatment W was living with his mother, and chose not to approach her with this information.

W was the oldest of four children. In his early youth his father deserted the family, and shortly thereafter his mother's physician allegedly advised her to 'get rid of one of those kids, for the sake of your health'. The oldest being the logical child to ship out, W was sent to live with relatives in his early adolescence. Later, his mother requested that he return, as she needed 'a man around the house.' During his treatment she informed him that she was ashamed to admit that a grown son was living under her roof, and that if he should ever move out she would never again open her door to him.

Although W raged against his mother in his sessions, his dependency inhibited any confrontations with her. In the transference, as well, he was careful not to express the hostility which at times was felt to simmer near the surface. More generally, he tended to idealize the female therapist. While this is less stressful for the therapist than work with the more abusive Vindictive Character, there are potential pitfalls. One of the difficulties in the therapy relationship with individuals such as W is the fact that in his isolation the patient often has no one but the therapist to fall back upon, and thus tends to suppress negative feelings in the transference. With W, displacement remained a major defense, as he ruminated about the Army chain of command in endless tirades, while raging near the surface about his mother's contemptuous treatment of him and daring not to express disappointment, deidealization, or, for that matter, wishes or feelings of attachment in the transference.

During the third year of treatment W purchased an automobile, to which he became extremely libidinally attached. His Chevrolet became a selfobject of immense importance, and such statements as 'I'd kill anyone who so much as dented a fender' were, needless to say, unsettling for the therapist. A test of his strengths and defenses occurred, though, when in a parking lot a driverless Volkswagen Beetle rolled into his treasured vehicle, not denting but scratching his fender. While watching and listening to this excruciating contact of metal, however, he discovered that the owner of the runaway automobile was an attractive young woman who stood by, watching helplessly and weeping, and announcing that this accident had happened on her very birthday. To his own astonishment, a gentle, warm side of W's personality emerged, as he responded by comforting the lady, compiling the information for an insurance report and proceeding to use the data to send her a belated birthday card.

Though W never again saw the owner of the heedless Volkswagen, the emergence of warm feelings in a moment of disaster marked a moment so significant to him that he later referred to the event as 'the hour when I came alive'. He was gradually able to dare to explore his positive and negative transferential feelings, and those in other relationships, as he became less consumed with vindictive rage directed, or misdirected, toward government agencies, laws and 'irresponsible hippies'.

Though B and W are presented as exemplifying the work with the Vindictive Character, and though there are many similarities in the etiologies of their personality disorders, there are clearly vast differences in the manner in which they were treated as children and in the ways in which they responded. Both were demeaned, dismissed and humiliated. Both were forced, for circumstantial reasons, to compete with siblings: B was compared with a deceased sister, while W was psychologically and literally banished for the reason that he was the oldest, and thus presumably the most self-reliant, and in fact the most expendable. Both were rejected by narcissistic parents; again, the dismissive attitude was far more subtle on the part of B's parents, who were preoccupied and had little time for their daughter, while W's mother was openly derisive and physically rejecting, locking him out of the house at the rapprochement stage of development and later, in early adolescence, farming him out to a relative and then reclaiming him at her convenience.

Both B and W reacted to denigrating parental treatment with hurt and intense resentment, evolving into vindictive, destructive rage in relationships in later years. Each may be described as *pan-angry*. Their anger, however, was expressed and directed in very dissimilar ways. B could be ruthless toward her contemporaries and sarcastic and cutting in the transference. W, intimidated by the abuse which he had experienced, tended to direct his outrage toward safer targets: the government and other institutions. In the transference he was inhibited in expressing negative feelings. As he became able to view the therapy relationship as a *safe* one, a rarity in his experience, for many months and to some extent throughout his treatment W was slow to express anger overtly, for fear of jeopardizing the alliance: a unique component in his troubled life.

Creativity derailed

In discussing the work with the Exploited-Repressive patient, it was seen that avenues of creativity, blocked by an addiction to grudges, may be opened with energies freed by some resolution, or working through, of those issues which brought the individual to seek treatment.

The vendettas of the Vindictive Character, on the other hand, whether or not they are enacted, may become so consuming that there is danger of his creativity being seriously compromised. As Werman has stated, 'The desire for revenge can so pervade the inner world of an individual as to become an obsessive and destructive force in that person's life. For a creative artist, such an idee fixe can go so far as to totally dominate his or her work, with ruinous results' (1993, p.301). Werman illustrates this concept in describing the destructive effects of vindictiveness in the life of the artist James Ensor, a contemporary of Edgar Allen Poe, whose polemics against eminent personages 'reached the height of...a rejection of humanity, coinciding with the waning of his creative talent' (p.304). Ensor's energies became involved in publicly deprecating other artists with intense misanthrophy. His critics were

> contemptuous of his work, [and] treated him as 'degenerate', 'neurotic' and 'inept'. Whatever bitterness, feelings of abandonment, and desire for retaliation had stored up as a child because of the lack of a secure, caring home and sense of belonging to a community, now found a fertile ground for expression and were displaced onto the art world. His subsequent work bore witness to both his sense of martyrdom and his compulsion to revenge himself on those whom he regarded as his oppressors and 'torturers'. (pp.310–311)

Salzman (1973) describes the obsessive-compulsive individual's need for certainty as a factor limiting his capacity for creativity (p.272). By the same token, the obsession with revenge can be not only limiting but destructive of the individual's imaginative powers. Unlike M, the Vindictive Character does not *deplore* his addiction to vengeful thinking: he *revels* in the experience of plotting and/or carrying out retaliation.

The case of G

G, a master's degree candidate at a prestigious university, sought psychiatric help, stating that she was a nervous wreck because of what one of her professors had done to her. Preparing himself to hear about real or fantasized seductive behavior, the therapist found his curiosity piqued as G continued with her account of academic injustice: the professor had given her a B!

G had planned to approach the president of the university with a complaint and an appeal. Her roommate, however, finding B furiously writing letters to the professor and to the president at three o'clock in the morning, 'not too gently suggested that I'd better see a shrink before I went any farther with it'.

G was the only daughter of five children of rigid and punitive parents, who offered G little support in her efforts to earn a master's degree in the humanities. Though they freely provided the college tuition for her brothers, two of whom were in precarious academic positions, G said that her parents had informed her that they saw no need for her to go to college, much less graduate school, 'because I'm only a girl, and I'd probably sooner or later get stuck with a bunch of kids anyway, just like my Mom, so what good would a college education do me?' Deeply enraged at their assessment of her worth, G had long since promised herself to show her parents just who in the family was worthwhile. She had determined throughout school and graduate school 'never to pull down anything less than an A'. This decision had limited her choices of course work, as she had consistently avoided 'anything that even smelled like hard science,' considering herself 'too right-brained to try to tackle anything with math in it'.

With diligence and a creative mind, G had managed never to earn less than the self-imposed A until she was faced with the fact that she could not complete her course work for the degree without taking a course in either statistics or physics. 'I chose physics,' she told her therapist, 'because I heard the statistics prof was tough and unforgiving. But you can't imagine what I've been through. With some tutoring, I managed to squeak by' (that is, making A's) 'until the midterm, and then it all blew up.' She received the grade of B.

'It just didn't belong to me,' she said. 'I had a feeling the exam papers had been collected before the allotted time, and so I went to the professor to talk about that, but he sort of shrugged me off, saying "You've just had a learning experience."' G considered dropping the course, but her advisor persuaded her to 'tough it out.' She began to note flaws in the physics professor's teaching methods. She asked questions which she felt were dismissed. She went to an administrative office to inquire about the professor's credentials but found that 'the girl behind the desk looked at me suspiciously, and so I left'.

G asked for permission to retake the examination, or to do extra work which would constitute the equivalent of a raise in her grade, bringing the average up to an A. When this effort was to no avail, she found herself losing sleep and writing angry letters which were never dispatched. Worse still, she recognized that she was becoming alienated from her major work, the proposal of her thesis, which had been highly praised by her advisor for its originality. G was never able to obliterate the B, a fact which in her eyes constituted both a devastating failure and a challenge to her equanimity and to her view of herself and her relationships. Several years later, a professional writer with a number of publications to her credit, G entered into psychoanalytic psychotherapy, realizing that there were many unresolved issues to be dealt with. Of her crisis in the graduate program, she said, 'If it hadn't been for an understanding advisor, a good therapist and a loyal roommate, I don't know where I would have ended up.' She had come to understand that she was in the grip of intense resentment toward her parents, expressed in a vendetta against a professor of physics who was the unwitting recipient of a monumental displaced rage, and that her not inconsiderable creative powers were in danger of being fatally submerged by her obsession with 'justice,' as she saw it.

'It wasn't a matter of justice at all,' she said in one of her early therapy sessions. 'It was a matter of getting even with my parents and my brothers, who thought nothing of putting me down. I was about to demolish myself trying to push them off their pedestals. Thank God for my roommate; she brought me back to earth when she said, 'Get real, G. Go see a shrink. You're going nuts just because you were stung by a B.'

Characteristics, problems and enticements in work with the Vindictive Character

Whereas the Exploited-Repressive patient presents with symptoms – mood or anxiety disorders, disorders of eating or sleeping, etc. – the Vindictive Character is likely to seek help in getting 'things' back on track. His lifestyle, perhaps, has been threatened. As his driving affect is often anger, he does not feel the emotional pain in the same way as the Exploited-Repressive patient, and thus there is not the same motivation for treatment and consequently for forming a therapeutic alliance.

In the evaluation phase of the treatment, the Vindictive Character may challenge the therapist in ways which make the latter uneasy. He may question the fee, or he may make requests for special consideration regarding issues such as time or frequency of appointments, in which case the therapist finds himself feeling protective of or defensive about his practices. When this occurs, negative transference and countertransference become factors at the very outset of the relationship.

Unlike the Exploited-Repressive patient, upon arrival in the therapist's office the Vindictive Character's agenda, conscious or unconscious, is likely to include revenge against the perpetrator of his humiliation or his defeat. He knows who slew him, whereas the Exploited-Repressive individual is less aware of the sources of his discomfort. The latter is asking for help in relieving his pain, while the Vindictive Character seeks tools to aid him in his efforts to slay his dragon.

The adjectives 'arrogant,' 'hopelessly inaccessible' and 'cynical' are commonly found in descriptions of this personality. Daniels (1967), in writing of the development of the Vindictive Character, states:

He zealously guards his independence and denies the possibility of ever needing anyone. Unlike the bully, he makes no attempt at outright domination of others; but his entrenched belief in his own superiority enables him unabashedly to humiliate, exploit, and frustrate many if not most of the people with whom he comes into contact. Cherishing his pride, he is sensitive and quick to take offense. Having done so, he is unremitting and unrelenting in his efforts to achieve revenge. (p.822)

In the interaction with the Vindictive Character, the therapist is more likely than the patient to be aware of his own anxiety. As stated by Glickauf-Hughes and Mehlman, 'Dealing with difficult clients who use projection, projective identification, and splitting, tests the limits even of individuals with resilient self-esteem' (1995, p.216). In discussing pathological vindictiveness, Daniels states: 'The vindictive character obviously constitutes a formidable problem for the psychoanalyst. Everything about him militates against trust, against mutuality, against help, against change' (1969, p.194).

Lane (1995), in describing the treatment process with the 'arrogant-vindictive patient,' states that 'Patients in whom vindictiveness is a central organizing force have a basic mistrust of people and therefore do not readily form a therapeutic alliance... Vengeful acting out will be especially likely when the patient makes a step forward in treatment' (p.56).

Horney (1936), in discussing the negative therapeutic reaction, reviews one of the most daunting hurdles in the work with the Vindictive Character. Referring to Freud's observations concerning this phenomenon, she states:

> This sequence of reactions is invariably present: first, a definite relief, then a shrinking back from the prospect of improvement, discouragement, doubts, hopelessness, wishes to break off... The impulse to berate the analyst more often comes out indirectly; doubts of the analyst; increasing complaints with a tendency to state that he is of no help...all indicating a hostility which may be so strong that if repressed it may show itself in suicidal ideas. (p.30)

Countertransference responses

Considering the Vindictive Character's arsenal of defenses, it is indeed a rare therapist who is able to meet his challenges with relative aplomb, and without some degree of negative countertransference. With regard to the negative therapeutic reaction, one of the most difficult components of work with the Vindictive Character, Olinick (1978) states: 'Every analyst has his threshold for countertransference reaction' (p.168). Addressing this issue, Lane (1985) states:

> Countertransference responses in the negative therapeutic reaction are probably greater than in other emotional disorders. The countertransference responses are reactions to the patient's sadism, his belittling of the analyst and

the analytic work, his arrogant narcissism, his provocativeness and seduct-
iveness, all designed to make the analyst into the hated and beloved introject.
(p.94)

Considering the negative qualities described above, it would be surprising if the
therapist did not find himself entertaining wishes to be free of the patient who is
so driven by vindictiveness. In fact, it is not uncommon for the therapist to hear,
among the early statements of the Vindictive Character: 'Dr X gave up on me' or 'I
thought Dr Y would take me, but he found his caseload was already too full.' Here
is the other side of the question 'When is enough enough?' The patient, with his
uncanny ability to provoke, may eventually cross the line of acceptable provocations and succeed in stirring up retaliatory responses in the therapist. If, for
example, after a confrontation he, the patient, should threaten to walk out and
never return, the therapist might well be tempted to say, in effect, 'Go ahead. Be
my guest.' When this happens, no matter how the therapist's message is expressed,
the patient will relive the early experiences that brought him to his present
predicament: abandonment, dismissal and scorn on the part of the individuals
upon whom he depends. He has, of course, been dismissive and scornful, and has
threatened to abandon his therapist, who may harbour a wish to retaliate in kind.

With some vindictive patients, it is possible to foresee this unfortunate juncture
in the treatment relationship and to provide the therapeutic cushion which is
afforded by carefully tailored structure-building and limit-setting. Put another
way, 'anticipate your battles.' Still, it must be stated that therapists, too, have their
limits, and it would be sanctimonious to suggest otherwise. With some patients,
no amount of wisdom and patience will be sufficient to prevent a rupture.

Some enticements

Considering the above representations of the Vindictive Character, a positive
countertransference would seem to be next to saintly. The patient is described in
predominantly negative terms. And yet there are therapists who greet this
challenging individual with some measure of enthusiasm. To some, not only is it
invigorating to have a certain number of difficult patients in one's practice, but
there is a certain stimulation in doing the detective work involved in working with
the Vindictive Character. Unlike the Exploited-Repressive patient, the etiology of
whose problems may be relatively apparent to the clinician at the evaluation stage
of treatment, the Vindictive Character, whose issue is that 'something is not
working,' does not wear his psychic background on his sleeve.

As has been proposed in the discussion of the work with the Exploited-
Repressive patient, the psychotherapist has often himself been subject to exploit-
ation, has become a conforming individual and fits easily into the role of helper.
The work is gratifying. On the whole, his work is appreciated. Yet he may himself

still have a few dragons of his own to slay; and if he accepts a Vindictive Character in treatment, he can admire if not identify with his patient's reckless aggressiveness and his ability, after horrendous confrontations with his antagonists, to walk off the stage without looking back. Admittedly, this is small reward for extraordinarily trying work. The motivations are there, however, there is no doubt about it. How else would we be learning, in quantum leaps, about the Vindictive Character, if the experts in our field were not willing to meet the challenges and share their experiences?

There may, in fact, be a certain allure to becoming acquainted with the problems of the Vindictive Character and his personality; in being privy to his outrage and his very vindictiveness. As Gabbard (1989) states of refractory, 'special' patients, 'These patients create extraordinarily intense countertransference reactions in treaters and come to occupy a favored position in the lives of their treaters. Although the 'special' patients may manifest transference hate that repels some treaters, they also inspire heroic rescue fantasies in other treaters, who will go to any length to help these patients' (p.96). Indeed, as McLaughlin (1961) reminds us, 'In any community of analysts it quickly becomes known to all that some are "wearers of the hair shirt" and will undertake difficult and demanding cases, and that others are oppositely self-protective in their case selection and technical approach' (p.117).

Our fascination with the Vindictive Character, our identification with the aggressor, is a powerful factor in the enduring quality of some of our greatest literature. Reading some of the most timeless children's literature, one may be astonished, as was Barreca (1995), to find 'how many [children's classics] were at their very hearts, tales of vindication and retribution.' Discussing 'the visceral satisfactions provided by the uncut versions of childhood stories,' she cites the climax of *Red Riding Hood*, in which 'the woodsman, rescuing Red and her grandmother, slices open the wolf with his hatchet.' She adds: 'Nobody can tell me that this grand finale didn't help sustain an apparently inborn appetite for revenge as a suitable payoff.' Barreca goes on to illustrate this statement by describing the wicked witch in *Hansel and Gretel* being cooked in the oven, and Snow White avenging herself against her stepmother by living 'a lifetime of happiness with a responsive man instead of a glaring mirror' (p.18).

The captivating nature of revenge in literature is nowhere so well illustrated as in the enduring popularity of Herman Melville's *Moby Dick* (1949), in which Captain Ahab, who, in the words of Kohut, is 'in the grip of interminable narcissistic rage' (1972, p.362), goes to his death attempting to avenge himself upon the Great White Whale, who robbed him of his leg. This, surely, is vindictiveness incarnate. Upon completing his great novel, Melville wrote to Nathaniel Hawthorne, 'I have written a wicked book.' The glee in this statement is unmistakable. Although Melville's masterpiece was not well received for several generations, today *Moby Dick* is listed first in a literary publishing company's brochure advertising 'the 100 Greatest Books Ever Written.' A Smithsonian Associates course on Melville's works was offered in 1997, with three classes devoted to *Moby Dick*. Harold Bloom (1986) describes one of America's leading literary critics, Captain Ahab, the 'bereaved monomaniac,' as 'the greatest of American hero-villains,' and *Moby Dick* as 'one of three candidates for our national epic' (p.6).

For the clinician, *Moby Dick* epitomizes vindictiveness. Horney (1950) cites the tale as a literary example of 'arrogant vindictiveness,' while Daniels (1967) states that in literature the vindictive character 'is exemplified – almost to the point of caricature – by such towering, vengeance-driven figures as Captain Ahab of Melville's *Moby Dick*' (p.822).

This macabre tale has endured through the generations not only because Melville was a consummate artist, capable of portraying the most devastating inner pain, anguish and conflict, but also because he draws the reader into the inner workings of a mind which is intriguing in its vindictiveness and horrifying in its obsession with revenge.

There is also a continuing interest in *Moby Dick*'s author, with several excellent biographies written in the 1990s, including two in 1996: *Herman Melville, A Biography, Volume 1, 1819–1851*, by Hershel Parker (1996), and *Melville, A Biography*, by Laurie Robertson-Lorant (1996). This fascination is fortunate for those interested in the psychodynamics of the individual whose creativity, talents and life experiences have combined to produce this classic. Reading his biographies, we learn that Melville suffered a severe trauma at the age of twelve, when his father became financially bankrupt and, burdened with debts and hopeless about his financial responsibilities, collapsed both physically and mentally and died a fortnight later, deranged and maniacal. This crisis left Melville with highly inappropriate responsibilities, grief over his beloved father's death and a very ambivalent relationship with a cold and domineering mother.

The family's suffering and his feelings of abandonment combined to create in Melville 'a knot intrinsicate of feelings – eagerness for adventure and shrinking from an unfriendly world, reluctance to leave his mother and sisters and an unacknowledged but irresistible longing to tear himself from their too intense embrace' (Arvin 1950). He set out to sea, eventually traveling the South Pacific, the setting of his best known work. 'Beneath Melville's characteristic gravity and reserve of manner .there was a tiger-pit of irritable and contradictory emotionality' (p.30).

Is there not a similar combination of qualities in the Vindictive Character which makes him at some level accessible to the psychotherapist, and, in some measure, at the same time appealing? 'A tiger-pit of irritable and *contradictory emotionality.*'

Melville announced that he had written a wicked book, and the book has endured. The author was able to portray the mind of an obsessional maniac, which fascinates us. And it is believed that it is this *experience of vicarious wickedness*, lent by the patient, which makes the work with the Vindictive Character challenging, intriguing and perhaps, in some therapeutic dyads, in spite of his celebrated arrogance, disdain and alleged poor motivation for change, even agreeable and exhilarating. *With all of his offensive, negative characteristics, the Vindictive Character may inject a shot of psychological adrenalin into the daily work of the therapist.* There may be a vicarious pleasure in entering into his world of conflict, and there may even be some envy of his ability to create mayhem, given that the therapist's role seems to be primarily one of *resolving* conflicts with some measure of orderliness.

The patient, after all, has not lived under the constraints imposed upon the therapist. Horney (1948) states that there is more to compulsive vindictiveness than defensiveness writing of 'another element which is so often present in vindictive impulses, fantasies, or actions: the excitement, the thrill, the passion. ... This quality of excitement, of passion, stems from the hope for or the sensation of a *vindictive triumph.*' This triumph she compares to 'Cinderella's dreams of the prince charming who will single her out'. Mother, sister, or companions, *then*, will realize how blind they have been toward her superior beauty and goodness. But she will not bear any grudge and in the bigness of her generous heart become their benefactress... To have power, to humiliate, to exploit, to frustrate, essentially means triumph' (p.9).

In choosing his profession, the psychotherapist has committed himself to the pursuit of self-knowledge and a certain personal discipline. The Vindictive Character often does not seem to be beholden to these strictures and ideals, and thus offers a therapist a new, often dangerous and usually maddening, but undoubtedly stimulating perspective.

Finally, it must be acknowledged that writing on the subject of the Vindictive Character offers a stimulation quite different from that of research and writing on the subject of the Exploited-Repressive patient. There is a certain tautness in the literature and in the reaction to reading about and discussing a wicked stepmother which is somehow missing in the pursuit of understanding the dynamics of a Little Dorrit.

CHAPTER 3

Forgiveness

'Forgiveness is in the air,' a colleague commented recently, noting that during one weekend, in the Washington, D.C. metropolitan area, there were two programs offered to mental health professionals entitled respectively, 'The Garden of Forgiveness: To Tend or Not to Tend?' and 'To Forgive? Or Not to Forgive?' In the same mail was an announcement of a workshop at the Spring Convention of the Virginia Psychological Association: 'Forgiveness: An Emerging Process in Facilitating Emotional Healing and Growth.'

Forgiveness is indeed in the air. In local, national and international arenas, as well as in our clinical work, we are asked to consider issues of forgiveness, pardon, apology and amnesty. In the context of the present writing, these issues will be considered primarily from the point of view of the therapist who in his work with the Exploited-Repressive patient and the Vindictive Character is dealing with issues of revenge. First, in setting the stage for a discussion of clinical issues, I would like to present a brief overview of the phenomena taking place in our culture at the end of the millennium, as it would seem that there is a similarity between the process of movement from revenge to forgiveness in a culture and that of the individual.

Forgiveness' renaissance

Concerning the Holocaust

A notable example of the individual's transition from a categorical view of forgiveness to a less absolute one is seen in the content of two speeches by Elie Wiesel, one of the most celebrated survivors of the Holocaust. Upon accepting the Congressional Gold Medal from President Ronald Reagan during ceremonies at the Bitburg Cemetery in the summer of 1985, Wiesel echoed the moral essayist Abe Rosenthal, who proclaimed, 'Forgive them not, Father, for they knew what they did.' Later, at the opening ceremony for the United States Holocaust Memorial Museum in Washington, D.C. commemorating the Jews who died during the Holocaust in World War II, Wiesel urged, 'Come and learn what human beings can do to other human beings. Learn the limits of humanity. Learn, and hope is possible. Forget, and despair is inevitable.' With these words, Wiesel does not exhort us to dwell obsessively or vengefully upon our injuries. Rather, he urges us to avoid a repetition of an unparalleled inhumanity by refusing to succumb to repression or denial (Durham 1990, pp.133–134).

Another expression of the attempt to resolve the anguished years of the Holocaust is seen in a statement by Greta Bergmann, a German–Jewish high-jumper who after having qualified for the 1936 Olympic Games was excluded by the Nazi Sports Office Director. Interviewed sixty years later about her feelings about this arbitrary action, Bergmann said, 'There comes a time when you have to stop [dwelling upon the atrocities].' Neither Bergmann nor Wiesel can be said to have *forgiven* their perpetrators, in a moralistic sense; yet each in their own way came to terms with their dilemmas by drawing upon their own resources.

Simon Wiesenthal, in *The Sunflower* (1976), offers a stunning example of our discomfort in assessing issues of forgiveness. In a concentration camp during the Holocaust, Wiesenthal relates an encounter with a dying young SS officer who confessed of unspeakable atrocities toward Jews and asked Wiesenthal for forgiveness, a request which Wiesenthal could not bring himself to grant. In *The Sunflower*, he describes his predicament, his continuing self-doubt concerning his reaction, and the responses of thirty-two mature individuals of a variety of religious and professional backgrounds to the question: 'What is your reaction to my refusal to forgive this dying perpetrator?'

It would be difficult to find a better example of ambivalence concerning the topic of forgiveness, and the ambiguity of the term. With few exceptions, Wiesenthal's respondents answered with cautious qualifications to an extraordinarily emotionally laden question.

Apartheid

Archbishop Desmond Tutu, in his efforts to achieve a free, nonracial South Africa through the creation of the Truth and Reconciliation Commission, has addressed issues of justice, vengeance and forgiveness as they relate to apartheid. Of asking perpetrators of racial atrocities to confess their crimes in return for amnesty, he states:

> There is no point exacting vengeance now, knowing it will cause future vengeance by the offspring of those we punish. Vengeance leads only to revenge... Vengeance destroys those it claims and those who become intoxicated with it. It seems clear that if we don't deal with deep conflicts, they don't disappear. You can't cover the cracks forever. Forgiveness is not nebulous, unpractical and idealistic. It is, in fact, thoroughly realistic. It's realpolitik in the long run. (1998, p.6)

'The Forgiveness Movement'

A very different perspective on forgiveness can be seen in a segment of ABC Television's *20/20*, aired in early January, 1997, entitled 'I Forgive You.' This presentation was featured as bringing to the viewers' attention a recent and innovative self-help movement, 'The Forgiveness Movement,' designed to counteract the destructive effects of vengeful feelings and vindictiveness. Interestingly, the first two of the three segments of this program were devoted to exposé of exploitations of human weakness, including experimentation with medication involving mentally ill patients and 'junk medicine' used in the treatment of nonexistent allergies.

Revenge was described by Regina Barreca, the author of *Sweet Revenge: The Wicked Delights of Getting Even* (1995), as 'an appetite, like chocolate, or sex'. It was generally acknowledged in this program that 'we' cringed at the idea of forgiveness, but that nevertheless, despite all of the anxieties involved, forgiveness was once again coming into its own, with national conferences and the emergence of a new direction in psychotherapy: *forgiveness therapy*.

These developments were illustrated by scenes which can only be described, in the patently subjective opinion of this writer, as *chilling demonstrations of warmth*. Two failing relationships were portrayed, each resolved by forgiveness. In both cases, the antagonistic parties were enjoined by the therapist to renounce their resentments and their bitterness, cease rehashing the offenses responsible for their rancor, own up to their own shortcomings, bury hurts and ask forgiveness for their own offences in the relationship.

Theoretically, none of these recommendations can be contested. The objection of this writer relates to the fact that they are easily seen as prescriptions, or formulae, imposed from the outside, with the implicit assumption that the offenses and the resulting resentments and grudges are buried, and *resolved through rituals*. Forgiveness is *recommended* as an undertaking which is not only healthy but *right*, and thus the neutrality which is the *sine qua non* of psychodynamically informed psychotherapy is lost.

In this program the entreaties to forgive were in turn soundly rebuked by Susan Forward, author of *Toxic Parents: Overcoming Their Hurtful Legacy and Reclaiming Your Life* (1989), who asserts that forgiveness can be *destructive*, as the victim does all of the work and sets himself up to be a doormat. According to Forward:

> One of the most dangerous things about forgiveness is that it undercuts your ability to let go of your pent-up emotions. How can you acknowledge your anger against a parent whom you've already forgiven? Responsibility can go only one of two places: outward, onto the people who have hurt you, or inward, into yourself. Someone's got to be responsible. So you may forgive

your *parents* but end up hating *yourself* all the more in exchange. I also noticed that many clients rushed to forgiveness to avoid much of the painful work of therapy. They believed that by forgiving they could find a shortcut to feeling better. A handful of them 'forgave', left therapy, and wound up sinking even deeper into depression or anxiety. (p.189)

Forward believes that people can forgive, 'but that they should do it at the conclusion – not at the beginning – of their emotional housecleaning – they need to stop diminishing or discounting the damage that was done to them. Too often "forgive and forget" means "pretend it didn't happen"' (p.180).

With the exception of Forward's dissenting opinion, the *20/20* segment decidedly entreated the practice of forgiveness and participation in 'forgiveness therapy.' An array of self-help books documenting the strength of 'The Forgiveness Movement' was shown. This writer perused a number of these books and found them in large part to contain guidelines, lessons and even exercises related to forgiveness. One, entitled *Forgiveness* (Simon and Simon 1990), is advertised with the words 'In this singular guide to spiritual healing, the Simons share their same time-tested six-stage program that forms the basis of their internationally known 'forgiveness workshops'. Another, *Forgive and Forget* (Smedes 1984), states on the jacket: 'Anyone can tap the power of forgiveness to achieve healthier relationships and peace of mind. *Forgive and Forget* explains and then takes us step by step through the four states of forgiveness: hurting, hating, healing and reconciliation.' These statements are included in the 'lessons of forgiveness.'

It is one thing for *20/20* to present issues of forgiveness as *either/or* – vengeance or forgiveness, forgiveness therapy versus Susan Forward – clinicians, on the other hand, will presumably consider the possibilities of change and resilience, and perhaps compromise, according to the strengths and resources of the patient.

Forgiveness at the news-stand

Few issues in our culture are met with such widely diverse attitudes as those concerning forgiveness. Children are often counseled to forgive, and do so perhaps in order to avoid further unpleasantness, often with little enthusiasm and little understanding of the words they are instructed to repeat. Perhaps this accounts for the fact that when later one begins to question some of our accepted concepts, there is such ambiguity concerning forgiveness. I have chosen to discuss three articles published in the flurry of new interest in the topic between November 1997 and April 1998.

An article in the *Washington Post* entitled 'Faith brings forgiveness in brutal carjacking' (Slevin 1998) describes the consternation of a pastor's parishioners concerning his forgiveness of two women who attacked him during a carjacking, which resulted in the amputation of a part of his lower leg. Not only did the pastor forgive his attackers: he asked his congregation to do the same. His parishioners, 'who fear his famously warm heart is leading him astray,' petitioned the judge who was scheduled to sentence the women, asking that the offenders be punished to the full extent of the law. The article suggests that the pastor's loyal flock considered his forgiveness to be impulsive, if not irresponsible and even dangerous.

In a January 1998 issue of *Parade Magazine*, a Sunday supplement of the *Washington Post*, an article appeared entitled 'He killed my child, but I don't want him to die' (Wallechinsky, p.4), describing some of the dynamics of a group of murder victims' family members who are opposed to capital punishment. Having experienced, for the most part, compelling revenge wishes, members of this group had found, in varying degrees, that the execution of the murderer would not help them to deal with their grief. One member, in an apparent epiphany, came to experience empathy and compassion for the killer, to the extent that he offered forgiveness and initiated a lively correspondence with his relative's murderer. This might be seen as his way of working through the mourning process; it seemed, indeed, to have totally redirected his energies.

Most of the members of this group did not advocate forgiveness, yet they did not feel that closure would be accomplished by the execution of the murderer. The object of their hatred would have been removed, but they would still not have dealt with their grief, which they apparently viewed as interminable, to be dealt with by each in his own way. This view is also expressed in an article regarding Frank McCourt, the author of *Angela's Ashes*, depicting his dismal childhood in Ireland. The past, McCourt stated in an interview, is not something to banish but something to be lived with. 'I don't go home any more,' he said, 'with a chip on my shoulder.' These attitudes seem to depict the mourning process without the *act* of forgiveness.

An article in the *APA Monitor*, the official publication of the American Psychological Association, entitled 'Forgiveness helps keep relationships steadfast' (Azar 1997, p.14) cites research indicating that 'people who forgive someone who has hurt them seem to reap significant mental health benefits.' If the victim is able to empathize with the perpetrator, one researcher found, forgiving can be liberating, while 'hostility and aggression are linked to a host of health problems.' The author's subtitle is: 'The human art of forgiveness is finally getting serious consideration by the scientific community.'

The therapist's encounters with questions of forgiveness

Forgiveness is seen by some as a cancellation of blame and resentment, while others think of it in terms of a slow truce-making. 'The Forgiveness Movement' holds a positive view of forgiveness. In other quarters forgiveness is seen as a symptom of weakness, or as a surrender. Many clinicians are cautious about approaching the subject; the issue of forgiveness, with its religious associations, seems to lie in an area where many would prefer not to tread. And yet, forgiveness is clearly in the air. In what ways, then, can the therapist best integrate this ancient and modern component into the work of psychotherapy?

A cautious approach to forgiveness

The uneasy association between forgiveness and morals, or religion, was underscored for this writer when she undertook some research in a public library system, where it was found that books included in the category of 'Revenge' were found in the stacks labeled 'Psychology/Self-Help' or 'Philosophy/Self-Help,' while books in the category of 'Forgiveness' were found under 'Philosophy/Self-Help' and 'Christian Theology.' However one might interpret this policy, for many individuals there is an inescapable *right-and-wrong* association with the word 'forgiveness.'

LaMothe, Arnold and Crane (1998), in an article entitled 'The penumbra of religious discourse,' discuss a research finding indicating that there is a relative absence of empathic inquiry regarding patients' religious experiences in psychoanalytic therapy. In asking, 'What does the omission of or lack of curiosity concerning religious language mean for the therapeutic relationship?', they conclude that:

> For the patient a therapist's selective attunement to or failure to recognize self-assertions of religious experience certainly has repercussions for transference-countertransference processes. The foreclosure of or restraints on bringing such experiences into the therapeutic relationship inevitably impose limits, as would the exclusions of any area of experience. (p.71)

Forgiveness scorned

The *appropriateness* of forgiveness as an issue in psychotherapy is disputed by Miller (1994) when she states:

> My own experience has taught me that the enactment of forgiveness – which, sixteen years ago, I still believed to be right – brings the therapeutic process to a halt. It *blocks* the unfolding of feelings and perceptions that are impossible to experience at the early stages of therapy, but that, with an increase of inner strength and resilience, can eventually be faced. Some memories surface years after the beginning of self-therapy, which we have finally become strong enough to face. This fruitful surfacing of new memories must not be hindered by the closure that forgiveness would produce. (p.21)

In perusing clinical articles on the subject of forgiveness, this writer observed that the authors often preceded their discussions with a disclaimer. Gartner, for example, speaks on this issue in remarking on 'the suspicion that many readers may share, namely, that [the topic of forgiveness]…is only important to those who, because of their own religious agenda, wish to call attention to religious concepts like forgiveness' (1992, p.21). Hunter states, even more explicitly, 'No resume of the meanings and uses of 'forgiving' would be complete without mentioning that sometimes the word can have about it an unctuous or smug quality, as though the forgiver is possessed of astonishing and irritating virtue' (1978, p.168). Citing Hunter's statement, Gartner comments that 'Those who have traveled in religious circles are no doubt familiar with this brand of compassion (p.24).

Forgiveness is seen by some writers as an easy way out for the victim. Referring primarily to victims of sexual abuse, Herman states:

> Revolted by the fantasy of revenge, some survivors attempt to bypass their outrage altogether through a fantasy of forgiveness. This fantasy, like its polar opposite, is an attempt at empowerment. The survivor imagines that she can transcend her rage and erase the impact of the trauma through a willed, defiant act of love. But it is not possible to exorcize the trauma, through either hatred or love. Like revenge, the fantasy of forgiveness often becomes a cruel torture, because it remains outside of reach for most ordinary human beings. Folk wisdom recognized that to forgive is divine. And even divine forgiveness, in most religious systems, is not unconditional. True forgiveness cannot be granted until the perpetrator has sought and earned it through confession, repentance, and restitution. (1992, pp.189–190)

It is intriguing to contemplate Herman's phrase 'a willed, defiant act of love.' To say, through clenched teeth, 'I forgive you,' usually effects little change in a relationship. If both recognize it as a false attempt at closure, the statement of forgiveness may increase the tension between perpetrator and victim. The forgiven party may, in fact, feel enraged or even dismissed by the unexpected offer of forgiveness. This response is colorfully illustrated by Margaret Atwood in *The Robber Bride* (1993), when at the height of an argument, Charis opens her mouth and astonishes even herself by saying to her antagonist, Zenia: 'I forgive you.' Zenia's response is to laugh angrily, saying, 'Who do you think you are? Why should I give a flying fuck whether you forgive me or not? Stuff your forgiveness!' (p.425).

Another amusing, tongue-in-cheek example of 'a willed, defiant act of love' is offered by Judith Martin, 'Miss Manners' in a post-Christmas column in the *Washington Post* (5 January 1997), under the heading, 'The season of sharing grief.' Martin advises writers who have been insulted or slighted in some way by 'loved ones' during the holidays to forget all these hurts and resolve to 'send all these people good wishes next year, with as much sincerity as possible.' But, she cautions, 'refrain from sending them presents.'

Miller describes forgiveness as a cowardly way out for the victim:

> Many writers try to escape the pain of their own childhood by preaching forgiveness, discipline, goodwill, and 'spirituality' to themselves and others, as though these practices could extinguish the truth stored in the body. But the body can't be deceived; it knows our true story very precisely. Intellectual generalizations cannot help us gain access to the secrets with which we have unconsciously lived for decades. Those secrets have first to be articulated via our feelings, because as infants who had to repress our pain and helpless rage, we were incapable of thinking: we could only feel. (1994, pp.14–15)

Pattison (1965) defines forgiveness as 'the completed act of reconciliation of the guilty one with the offended one,' optimally resulting in mutual acceptance and reconciliation. 'Pathological failures of forgiveness,' he states, 'occur at each step of this process... Failures in mutual acceptance include demanding the 'pound of flesh' as a condition of forgiveness, or a condescending gesture of forgiving as a duty. In either case, the forgiveness is a façade. It is a receipt of payment, but it is not reconciliation' (pp.112–114).

Forgiveness as part of the healing process: Mourning revisited

Considering the above attitudes toward forgiveness, ranging from controversial to censorious, it is interesting and somewhat puzzling that forgiveness as a concept and as a process is beginning to be reconsidered from a more positive perspective.

When seen in connection with the healing process for the victim, forgiveness may be looked upon as an intrinsic, positive part of *mourning the passage of revenge*. Freud, in 'Mourning and melancholia' (1959, p.256), described mourning as 'detaching the libido bit by bit;' and it is this very process which characterizes forgiveness, in the true sense of the word. In a previous work, this writer addressed this issue in stating:

> The *ongoing process of forgiving*...[is] a process which takes time, often protracted time, and which requires immense effort on the part of the forgiving one. This effort may comprise a major portion of the process of the work with the narcissistically wounded client, and...is *akin to the work of mourning*... Relinquishing vengefulness means forfeiting pride or malice, and perhaps also letting go of an unhealthy attachment. In the psychological sense, forgiveness is not an act which takes place when anger or hurt or revenge are spent. Rather, it involves the introduction of a leavening agent, an amalgamation resulting in something new: a solution. (Durham 1990, pp.134–135)

Hunter (1978) elucidates the distinction between *forgetting* and the process of *forgiving* in stating:

> Of particular significance for the psychology of forgiving are the phrases 'let bygones be bygones', 'forgive and forget', and 'think no more of it'. Thus, forgetting is an almost invariable accompaniment of forgiving, and forgiving leads to it, the process not being complete unless forgetting results. This is literally forgetting and not repressing, and is analogous to the letting go and forgetting that takes place through mourning. (p.167)

In describing the relationship between forgiveness and grief and mourning, he states:

> They are not the same processes, although in certain situations forgiveness may lead to mourning (the giving up of an old object) or mourning may lead to forgiveness... The differences are as follows: forgiveness has to do primarily with the psychodynamics of aggression, not grief. In forgiveness there is no necessary object loss. In forgiveness a resented object becomes an accepted object. In forgiveness the angry affect changes to a rueful or regretful one, not a grieving one. An important similarity, however, is that both forgiveness and mourning result in an eventual decathexis of the object. (p.172)

Referring to the potential healing qualities of forgiveness, Barreca, in *Sweet Revenge: The Wicked Delights of Getting Even*, depicts the relationship between revenge and forgiveness thus:

> Letting go of the pain inflicted by someone else does not have to be motivated by any desire whatsoever to allow that other person off the hook – in order to achieve a fresh beginning there must be a sense of a threshold crossed, of being able to stamp 'paid' on the debts stockpiled by the suffering and anger of the past. Getting even can mean getting on with a life that is not informed by anger, resentments, or old, unsettled scores but is instead about perspective, justice and the possibilities of forgiveness. (1996, p.246)

Apologies

As the question of forgiveness gains momentum in worldwide forums, the question of apology raises further issues. How is the act of apology received by the individual, group or nation that has been offended, wronged, sinned against? Under what circumstances is an apology seen as real: as acceptable?

H says 'I'm sorry': When an apology is seen as perfunctory

J, an anxious, accommodating woman in her late thirties, arrived for her therapy session in apparent anguish after a camping vacation, which she had hoped would strengthen her relationship with H, a somewhat overbearing man about whom she had for months felt ambivalent. J and H both enjoyed wilderness holidays and had spent days preparing. Both were divorced and each had hoped to find a congenial partner for what J called 'a second try'.

'He treated me like his flunky' was J's opening statement to her therapist. 'He didn't give a thought to my comfort or safety; several times he wandered off and left me alone in the forest, and wondered why I was shaking when he came back.' Although they had planned to share the responsibilities of camping – setting up the tent, preparing the campfire and the meals – each evening when they returned to their campsite, H had gone inside the tent to relax while J built the campfire and cooked the meals. She frequently found him asleep when dinner was ready, and when he woke 'it was as though a servant had delivered the food. He gobbled his dinner with hardly a comment.' In their isolated situation J was reluctant to express her grief and disappointment about H's demeaning behavior and attitude; 'I kept my counsel,' she said. 'I blame myself for not speaking up, but I was sort of afraid to. All the way home I kept quiet. I decided he'd failed the test, and I was ready to break off the relationship, but I didn't want to get into a lot of unpleasantness on the long ride home, so I just stayed quiet.

'Then we went our own ways,' she continued. 'And I've never been so disillusioned and depressed. Then a few days later, H dropped by my office, walked in, sat on the edge of my desk and said "The meals were great!" I couldn't believe how offhand he was. Then he said "Oh, sorry about the naps." That was supposed to make everything all right, and he said "See you!" and left. *Two words* were supposed to clear the slate.'

J, clearly the epitome of the Exploited-Repressive individual, was embarrassed to describe to her therapist the scenarios of the fateful camping trip. She had in fact not shared the details of the week with her friends and colleagues, as the natural response would have been, 'Why didn't you tell the jackass to go to hell?' She did not challenge H for the very reason that had brought her to therapy: she was anxious, timid and self-effacing, and it was not in her nature to protest against even the most egregious exploitation. Though she had begun to be aware of her tendency to allow herself to be used, and, as she put it, was 'taking some small steps toward respecting myself,' she did not have the courage, in the isolation of the forest, to make an issue of her companion's unseemly, insulting behavior.

'When the week was over, I hated him,' she said, 'and I hated myself too. But it wasn't until that breezy "Oh, sorry" that I felt that I really could have wrung his neck. He must have thought I had no self respect at all, that I would forgive and forget because he tossed out a couple of words. If he had even said "Give me another chance, I'll try to make it up to you," it would be different.'

A perfunctory apology, then, can be more of an affront than no apology at all. For H, the glib 'sorry' brought about a quite unintended reaction: it inflamed the individual whom it was intended to pacify.

Some public apologies

The word 'apology' has in fact gained both respect and contempt in recent months, as it has become associated with an effort on the part of certain government personnel to achieve closure on the issue of slavery in United States history. In the early summer of 1997, a congressional representative broached the idea of a congressional apology for slavery as a simple and moral starting point in the effort to heal the nation's racial wounds. Reviewing the reactions to this proposition ten months after it was made public, it is difficult to find comments *in the press* which are not clearly scornful. An article in *Time* (by Walter Shapiro, 30 June 1997) speaks of 'the current Age of Apology... Now Congress has embraced contrition chic' (p.18). In the same issue, there is an article by Jack E. White entitled 'Sorry isn't good enough: A simple apology for slavery leaves unpaid debts.' Later, a *Washington Post* article by Michael A. Fletcher (5 August 1997) appeared under the headline 'For Americans nothing is simple about making [an] apology for slavery: The congressman's suggestion draws fire from all sides'. In December 1997, *Newsweek* featured two articles on the burgeoning interest in slavery. The first, 'The long shadow of slavery,' on Steven Spielberg's film *Amistad*, states: 'An important new movie, and a fresh debate over a national apology, show that even after more than a century America's "original sin" still haunts the national psyche' (Alter 1997, p.58). The second article (Ellis Cose, p.68) criticizes the suggestion that a slave memorial be erected on the Washington Mall. 'There are limits,' the author states, 'to the extent to which one can correct for past wrongs. One may have to make peace with the past.'

Jonathan Yardley, reviewing Edward Ball's *Slaves in the Family* in *The Washington Post Book World* (22 February 1998) offers a scathing commentary on 'the age of apology':

> All of a sudden, for reasons difficult to pin down, slavery is too much with us. A nation that for most of its existence preferred to ignore or gloss over the most indelible stain on its good name now cannot get enough of it. Public figures from the president on down make a great show of agonizing over whether a formal 'apology' for slavery should be issued... 'Apologizing for the country's past can only gratify the apologizer's desire to feel good about himself', Russell Baker wrote last summer as the apology movement gained steam '...It not only enhances the apologizer's self-esteem. It doesn't cost him anything.' That, in a nutshell, is why the apology movement is ultimately both frivolous and pointless. (p.3)

It will be noted that the discussions of 'the apology movement' are directed almost exclusively toward the perpetrator (or his progeny), with little exploration of the reactions of the victims or their descendants. Yet, an important question is: *how does the apologee feel?* This, of course, is a primary question for the therapist whose patient is dealing with issues of revenge and forgiveness. An apology, of course, may be well-meant and welcomed by the patient. If, however, his perpetrator should approach him with a request for pardon which appears to be little more than a self-serving ploy, as many of the above apologies are purported to be, will the patient feel, as did J after her dismal camping trip with H, twice offended?

Often he will. In some circumstances he may, however, derive some gratification from being in the position of *deciding the outcome of a conflict*. He can exact revenge by refusing to accept the apology. To the individual who feels dismissed or denigrated, who feels that he has in some way lost autonomy, an apology may thus have a paradoxical effect: he is at last in some control of the situation. Although refusing an offer of apology does not have the effect of undoing the damage incurred, it may provide some satisfaction which is not otherwise available to him. To be grateful, on the other hand – to accept an apology, to 'wipe the slate clean' – may to him be tantamount to being obliterated from further consideration.

When an apology is seen as a step toward reparation

If during their camping trip H had said: 'J, I'm sorry about the way I've been treating you, running off and leaving you alone, and I know the mealtimes must have been awful for you. I want to make up for it. I'll quit konking out before dinner, and I'll help you with the meal,' J might have felt that he was considering her feelings. She might have acknowledged that she was angry and hurt, clearing the air and giving the holiday and the relationship a second chance. H's apology, however, given long after the holiday, seemed self-serving and perfunctory, carrying with it the assumption that he owed no more than a few words.

Forgiveness and hatred

'To hate,' states Galdston (1987), 'is the opposite of love, a condition of ill will, malevolence held over time... It is both an emotion and a mental activity that contains the desire for revenge' (p.371).

We are accustomed to viewing hate as a negative, destructive emotion which must be overcome if forgiveness is to be attained ('Love your enemies'). And of course hatred can be totally destructive: one has only to consider the Holocaust and the hate crimes throughout our nation. However, some degree of hatred is inevitable, and it may be looked upon as an ingredient in the Individual's emotions which, as Blum (1997) states, 'may also subserve adaptation and personality organization.' To this end, it is interesting to examine some ways in which expressions of hatred may serve usefully in the treatment of both the Exploited-Repressive individual and the Vindictive Character.

First, it is important to note the distinction between hatred and rage. According to Kernberg (1994):

> Hatred, I propose, is a complex, structured derivative of rage, that expresses the combined wishes to destroy a bad object, to make it suffer, and to control it on the part of an enraged self. In contrast to the acute, transitory, and disruptive quality of rage, it is a chronic, stable, usually characterologically anchored affect. The object relationship framing this affect expresses concretely the desire to destroy or dominate the object. An almost unavoidable consequence of hatred is its justification as a revenge against the frustrating object, and revengefulness is a typical characterological form of hatred. (p.705)

An expression of rage does not necessarily imply a wish for revenge. Rage may be all-consuming for a moment, and may soon dissipate. Hatred, too, however, can be *all-consuming*; hatred often cannot be overcome without professional help. As Galdston states it, 'The patient cannot get over…[hatred] alone because hatred binds him to an object from the past in the grip of an ancient grudge that requires transference for its release' (1987, p.375).

The above two statements are not contradictory when viewed within the framework of Galdston's proposed three categories of 'competence to hate' (p.371): those individuals 'who are unable to hate, those who cannot stop hating and those who have learned both how to hate and how to get over hating.' It is those in the third category, of course, who are able to forgive. And according to the formulation of categories in the present writing, the difficulties of the first 'variety' of individuals – those who are unable to hate – correspond to the Exploited-Repressive individual, while those in the second category – those who cannot stop hating – fit the definition of the Vindictive Character. Blum (1997) makes this distinction between the two categories of 'competence to hate' in stating: 'Just as untamed hate is pathological, so is the inability to consciously hate or to relinquish hate. When hate cannot be appropriately expressed, it tends to go underground, often leading to somatization and self-hatred' (p.364). The challenge of the therapist, then, is to help his patient, either the Exploited-Repressive individual or the Vindictive Character, to be aware of his hatred, to temper it and, in Galdston's words, to 'detach aggression from the obligatory pursuit of an object lost through disappointment and to retrieve energy for new endeavors.'

The Exploited-Repressive patient, as he begins to become aware of the ways in which he has been used by his parents or other significant persons, will often react by *hating himself*. It is humiliating to realize that one has allowed oneself to be exploited. As noted in the case of L, in work with the exploited patient shame in the transference, which may lead to self-loathing, creates the danger of premature termination. Thus the patient, who has become 'able to hate,' must deal with the emergence of self-hate and hatred toward his perpetrator, and likely very ambivalent feelings toward the therapist who has been his 'accomplice' in the process of excavating his hatred and rage. The exploration of the transference responses, then, are essential to the resolution of his conflicts and the possibilities of forgiveness.

Hatred toward the exploiter, or the perpetrator, may be expressed unconsciously by the Exploited-Repressive individual in *excessive concern for the perpetrator*, usually the parent. This concern, according to Pick (1995), 'while partly related to a real wish for reparation, simultaneously shows itself to be a reaction formation against an attitude of hostility and superiority towards the object' (p.257). This hostility is expressed in subtle ways: most characteristically, in overweening concern about the welfare of a negligent or indifferent parent. In Pick's words:

> These patients unconsciously feel neglected and abused. In vengeful hatred and desperation, as well as envious rivalry, they at the same time project hatred into the 'breast' (or some aspect of 'mother') and appropriate it, become it. This occurs not in a loving way nor in a loving identification with a good breast, but in part at least in a hateful way, in identification with a fundamentally cruel, depriving breast. So while they may become 'mother', it is a mother secretly or unconsciously filled with hatred. (p.258)

Neither the patient who hates himself nor the patient who shows spurious concern for the other is actually 'unable to hate,' but is not conscious of the way in which his hatred is expressed. And again, it is primarily through the transference that his unconscious antipathies will be expressed.

In work with the Vindictive Character who 'cannot stop hating,' the therapist may be in the position of dealing with the addictive quality of chronic hatred, which is often manifested early in the transference.

The tendency toward splitting, characteristic of the vindictive borderline individual, often precludes the possibility of forgiveness. If there is a rupture in the therapeutic relationship before forgiveness can be considered, the patient is likely to terminate the relationship abruptly, precluding the question of forgiveness. It is as though he says to the therapist: 'One strike and you're out.' One of the tragedies of work with the Vindictive Character, then, is that hatred and vengefulness remain powerful motivating factors, and even those relationships which seem promising may be truncated without notice and without a chance of reconciliation, as in the patient's eyes 'all good' can precipitously become 'no good.'

On a more positive note, Gartner (1992) indicates that in the work with the vindictive borderline patient, if the therapist can tolerate the patient's aggression without retaliating or withdrawing, the process of healing and integrating can occur. 'The ability of the therapeutic relationship to endure hate and aggression,' he states, 'serves as a living contradiction to the notion that either the patient or the therapist is "all bad". It is this living witness to the reality of ambivalence that makes the capacity for forgiveness possible' (p.27).

In offering an operational definition of forgiveness, Gartner states that 'Mature forgiveness is definitely not the replacement of negative hateful feelings with loving feelings, as is commonly believed' (p.23). On the other hand, Galdston (1987) states that:

> It is my contention that the development of the abilities to hate and *to get over hating* are two major accomplishments in the ego's growth toward the mastery of aggression in relating to the object world. Hatred can lead to forgiving the trespasser, foregoing revenge and forgetting the offence. By letting bygones be bygones the ego is enabled to detach aggression from the obligatory pursuit of an object lost through disappointment and to retrieve energy for new endeavors. (p.371; my italic)

If the statements of Gartner and Galdston seem contradictory, the word *replacement* in Gartner's phrasing would seem to be the key to their confluence. Both agree that the goal of therapy is not to 'cancel' hateful feelings and instill love, but to render the powerful hatred less potent by helping the patient to redirect his energies. In so doing, the 'bygones' lose their grip and the patient's horizons broaden. In the work with the vindictive borderline patient, this aspect of the work is extraordinarily challenging. As Wolberg (1979) states, 'Success or failure in the psychoanalytic treatment of the borderline is largely dependent upon the adequacy of the working through process. This is difficult and time consuming because of the volatility of emotions and the complicated network of defenses' (p.235). Compounding the difficulties is the often intense transference and countertransference hatred. However, as Galdston expresses it, 'By agreeing to be exposed to hatred the analyst affords the patient an opportunity to capture the particulars of his hatred and to identify the sources of frustration and disappointment that compel his need to seek revenge' (1987, p.375).

For the best summary of the relationship between hatred and forgiveness, I turn again to Galdston, who concludes with the following statement:

> In addition to the work of mourning to retrieve the lost libido, the patient must do the work of hating, to liberate his aggression from continued service

to the past. Forgiveness is accomplished by recovering the aggression which had been pre-empted by the desire for revenge and redirecting it towards a new goal. The work of forgiving allows for the symbolic blending of aggression and libido into an endeavor created to replace a hated object. With forgiveness, the blocking introject loses its significance. The goal of revenge passes. Comfort in a stronger ego allows the patient the prospect of a future freed of hatred from the past. (1987, p.377)

CHAPTER 4

Encounters with Revenge in Child and Adolescent Psychotherapy

The two faces of revenge in children and adolescents

In considering the work of psychotherapy with young children, we are accustomed to thinking of revenge in terms of the aggressive, vindictive child who reacts to affronts or perceived affronts to his sense of himself by striking back or by hitting *before* he is hit. In this chapter I will address the difficulties of working with both the aggressive child and the repressive youngster, who is also likely to exact revenge upon his parents through symptom formation: eating disorders, encopresis, or school refusal, any of which may be his indirect way of saying 'I'll show you!' A consideration of a *revenge ingredient* in the child's symptoms may lead to a fruitful exploration of pathogenesis in work with young children and adolescents.

First, we must ask: In what ways does the child say 'I'll show you!'? How does he express himself to his parents and to his therapist? And how are the aggressive child and the repressive youngster perceived by the therapist? It should be noted at this point that when considering personality or temperament, the categorization of *aggressive/repressive* does not imply an either/or formulation. The division into types is made for economy of presentation, with the understanding that there may be considerable overlap in the child's response to difficult and anxiety-provoking situations.

At an Open House at a treatment center for disturbed children, I recall being met by a staff representative who in the course of her introductory remarks added the statement, 'We have a few openings at the present; and we're looking for the more quiet, depressed child.'

This remarkably unguarded statement expressed a universal, if unacknowledged preference on the part of child and adolescent therapists: the understandable preference for the subdued, agreeable patient. The child need not be *depressed*, as was specified at the Open House; however, the repressive youngster is, for many therapists, the patient of choice. Unless he is more able to be selective with his case load than is customary, however, the child therapist will deal with both aggressive and repressive children, and will consequently face clearly different challenges.

We are often aware early of the source of conflict in the aggressive child – the child who torments his younger sibling or aims a rock at a window – whereas we may have a mystery on our hands when exploring the source of the symptom formation in the child who refuses to eat, or who will not speak to persons outside of his family circle. Thus, with the aggressive child the therapist may find himself in the role of policeman, guarding himself or his office against verbal or literal attack, whereas in work with the repressive child he will more likely be called upon to sharpen his skills as a detective in order to uncover the underlying source of the child's symptoms. However enthusiastically we may welcome challenges, there is little doubt as to the relative appeal of the roles described here: policeman (or guard) or detective. We did not, after all, work for an advanced degree in order to learn to cope with a youngster who spits on our desk or who uses four-letter words to describe our person or our services.

Before discussing revenge as it relates to work with the aggressive child and the child who internalizes, some thoughts about temperament will be considered.

The question of temperament

Winnicott stated:

> It is wise to assume that fundamentally all individuals are essentially alike, and this in spite of the hereditary factors which make us what we are and make us individually distinct... One infant may tend to be aggressive and another may seem to show hardly any aggressiveness from the beginning; yet each has the same problem. It is simply that the two children are dealing with their load of aggressive impulses in different ways. (1984, p.93)

The classic studies of temperament are those of Thomas and Chess (1968; 1977; 1980) based upon their New York Longitudinal Study, begun in 1956, following 136 subjects from middle-class, native-born families from infancy into early adult life in 'a systematic study of individual differences, or temperament, in early infancy and their significance for the developmental process' (1980, p.70).

Three temperamental constellations were defined, and were given refreshingly jargon-free names: the 'Easy Child pattern,' the 'Difficult Child pattern' and the 'Slow-to-Warm-Up Child'. The authors conclude that 'Individual differences in temperament, as they are manifested in early infancy, may be the result of the interplay of genetic, prenatal, and early postnatal factors' (1980, p.75). As for the significance of temperament in the study of behavior disorders, throughout their reports on their findings the authors remind the reader that:

> A one-sided emphasis on temperament would...be antithetical to our view-point, which insists that we recognize temperament as only one attribute of

the organism .. The relevance of the concept of temperament to general psychiatric theory lies neither in its sole pertinence for behavior disorders, nor in its displacement of other conceptualizations, but in the fact that it must be incorporated into any general theory of normal and aberrant behavioral development if the theory is to be complete. (1968, p.183)

Thomas and Chess's studies are intriguing to professionals and laymen alike, as there is an undeniable fascination regarding individual differences in temperament, especially as seen in very young children. Noam Shpancer refers to 'individual differences in talent, emotional stability, and so on,' as '*the last remaining mystery*' (1997, p.1243, my italics). This mystery, of course, has long intrigued us, and has recently been explored by Winifred Gallagher, in her book, *I.D: How Heredity and Experience Make You Who You Are* (1996).

Gallagher begins her book with the gripping story of Monica, in a chapter entitled 'A dynamite smile.' Monica exhibited both self-protective withdrawal and 'innate magnetism,' emerging as an individual inspiring the statement, 'Contradicting the experts' dire predictions at nearly every turn, her life celebrates our often-underestimated resilience and demonstrates that even the harshest experience can add depth and luster to who we are' (p.11).

Monica's resilience illustrates 'the psychologically invulnerable child,' as described by Anthony, who states:

> A super child may come out of the ghetto and a sad and sorry child from the well-to-do suburbs. Why and how? By what mysterious process of psychological selection is the one destroyed and the other preserved? Admittedly, the two worlds may not be so different beneath the surface; a seemingly indulgent household in a superior neighborhood may camouflage as many cruelties and crudities as an overcrowded tenement apartment. Exposure is clearly not the whole story; vulnerability and mastery also play integral roles in determining the response to stress. (1974, p.533)

The question of appeal

Most adults are likely to be drawn to children like Monica, whose battles and temperament are impressive: indeed, humbling. Garmezy (1983) writes of protective factors in children that ameliorate their risk status, including 'temperament factors of a positive sort (e.g. flexibility of response, a positive mood). On the other hand, a child may be seen to be temperamentally shy, excitable, tense or laconic, in which case his parents' reactions to his disposition will vary according to their own personality configurations; and the same will be true of the attitude of his therapist, unless the latter is miraculously immune to preferences in his attitudes toward his patients.

The child who is of a timid disposition may be a disappointment to his parent, who urges him to be more aggressive and subtly or openly shames him for his reluctance to behave in a way more compatible with their own ideals. The child, in turn, may respond by making his parents' as well as his own life miserable by refusing to eat or by exhibiting phobias. The inherently aggressive child, on the other hand, may bring upon himself the wrath of parents who value decorum and gentility by responding to their coercion with vengeful efforts to show them who is boss.

The question of appeal and therapeutic 'match' will be considered more fully in a discussion of countertransference in child and adolescent therapy.

Revenge and the aggressive child

Though the word may have negative connotations, to characterize a child as 'aggressive' is not necessarily to impugn him. The aggressive child may be the delight of everyone in his orbit; he may be loving and considerate and at the same time forceful and eager for a fight. *Webster's Dictionary II* has two quite different definitions for the word 'aggressive': first, the adjectives 'hostile, combative,' followed by 'energetic and enterprising' and finally 'boldly assertive.' Clearly, in psychoanalytic thinking the first description is negative, while the following describe desirable qualities. Parens (1979) distinguishes between *destructive* and *nondestructive* aggression; in the latter, 'the aim is not destruction of self, object, or environment, but rather their control, assimilation, and mastery' (p.100). Hostile destructiveness, in Parens' framework, 'is not inborn; rather, it is provoked in the self by experience' (1991, p.81). He proposes that '*excessive* unpleasure of any source, not only frustration, generates hostile destructiveness even in early childhood' (p.83). If the child's primary caretakers have failed to protect him against excessive pain, then hostile destructiveness will develop. 'Hostile destructive affects,' Parens concludes, 'from irritability to anger, hostility, hate, and rage, develop progressively during the first three years of life. These beginnings are determined by the confluence of innate dispositions in interaction with experiences in the earliest relationships' (p.102). This statement is consistent with that of Rank (1949), whose work with aggressive children leads her to the conclusion that 'We do not conceive of aggression as an *unmodifiable innate* force of destruction' (p.47).

Parens' 'destructive aggression' seems to correspond to Winnicott's 'clinical aggression,' or 'something that cannot be encompassed,' as compared with 'inborn aggression,' which 'must be variable in a quantitative sense in the same way that everything else that is inherited is variable as between individuals' (1971, p.93). This view of the aggressive component in personality as inborn is supported by McGuire (1997) in his review of his findings regarding the stability of aggressiveness from childhood through adolescence and into young adulthood (pp.68–69).

It is the child who is clinically, or destructively, aggressive who is our concern in this writing: the vindictive child who lashes out, openly and directly, out of rage and hate, and a desire for revenge. In a work in progress at the time of this writing, *Roots of Prejudice,* Parens states, 'experiences of excessive unpleasure organize into how hostile destructive an individual one becomes,' concluding that 'those more heavily traumatized' are led to 'the unyielding need for retribution against "traumatizing others", of any kind, and even for revenge. There is more or less constant pressure to seek an object for this retribution/revenge.'

The preschool experiences of Ralph illustrate the characteristics of the clinically aggressive or hostile destructive child.

Ralph: 'With malice aforethought'

Ralph was three years of age when he was enrolled in a preschool for inner city children in a large metropolitan area. A sturdy child, Ralph was larger than many of the other three-year-old children in his group. From the beginning of the school year Ralph was identified as a very angry and intimidating bully. On the playground he would often be seen standing in front of a child who was riding a tricycle, his arms crossed, glaring at the rider. If the child protested at Ralph's blocking of his path, he or she was likely to be hit or pushed off the tricycle and onto the ground. This behavior often occurred even when there was a free tricycle nearby.

Ralph grabbed his classmates' toys, crayons and snacks. He was regularly given 'time out,' which he protested against with angry scowls and often abusive language toward teachers and classmates alike. Needless to say, the other children avoided Ralph, and his teachers often despaired in their efforts to 'civilize' his behavior.

Ralph's mother, a large, forbidding single woman, expressed puzzlement as to the roots of her son's behavior. It was not until a crisis occurred, involving the threat of expulsion, that she was able to offer information suggesting the genesis of Ralph's unacceptable behavior. For no apparent reason, Ralph had scratched the face of one of his classmates as she rested during nap time. Following this episode, at a crisis meeting with the faculty, Ralph's mother was able to reveal the information that a sister, Sophie, eight years older than Ralph, had from the time of his birth abused her brother physically and emotionally. As an example, when Ralph was given a tricycle for his third birthday, the sister had immediately begun methodically to push him off the new three-wheeler and onto the sidewalk, leaving him screaming and bleeding. His mother's solution to this problem was to give the tricycle to a cousin.

After a number of meetings on Ralph's behavior and the choice of an appropriate preschool placement, his mother was able to reveal that during Sophie's early years she, the mother, had regularly used drugs, to the extent that she was required to spend several months on a drug rehabilitation program, leaving her daughter in the care of an assortment of friends and relatives. She was unable to recall many features of her daughter's latency years, except to conclude, as she put it, that 'she was pretty much of a mess.'

It became clear, then, that Ralph's rage against his sister and his mother was being vented in the preschool setting, and his wrath and his desire for revenge displaced onto his classmates. He expressed old pain and frustration by treating smaller and less aggressive children in the way in which he had been treated. His anger was not openly directed toward his mother, an intimidating individual herself, but indirectly toward the nursery school staff, whom he may have perceived as helpless to control him, since the staff were under strictures regarding the discipline allowed with the small children in their charge.

Lane (1986) speaks of the psychogenesis of vindictiveness in the child, in stating:

> The wish for revenge has its roots in early mismatches between mother and infant. The caretaker fails to pick up the infant's cues, the child does not respond, is not nurtured, and the mismatch is neither recognized nor repaired... Mistrust and helplessness develop along with the inability to tolerate frustration. ... The child's narcissism is disturbed and their sense of omnipotence challenged too early, with a battle for control between parent and child ensuing very early in life. (p.48)

Ralph's sister, Sophie, had received little if any nurturance from her mother, and it seems that there was also a failure on the mother's part to pick up Ralph's cues, as seen in her response to Sophie's brutality toward her young brother: to get rid of his new tricycle rather than discipline the perpetrator of his pain.

Ralph appeared to the staff of his preschool to be 'primed for attack' when he arrived at school. He would stand on the periphery of the group, his eyes narrowed, appearing to be choosing a target for attack. This is quite different from the behavior of the child who suddenly and unpredictably explodes into a tantrum. One of Ralph's classmates, Danny, might arrive at the center with a hug for his teacher and a smile on his face, only to burst into uncontrolled rage a few moments later when someone snatched a toy from him. Danny, like Ralph, had suffered from neglect and abandonment on the part of a substance-abusing caregiver, the details of which were not made clear, but which had left devastating psychological traces. Perhaps because of the nature of the abuse and perhaps because of factors of temperament, Danny had emerged with what Rank (1949) describes as a 'fragmented ego', and 'a very low threshold of tolerance for frustration which, in turn, produces constant tension and/or anxiety. The tension and/or anxiety finds its primary expression in a motor-expressive discharge' (p.43).

Both Ralph and Danny displayed intensely aggressive behavior. Ralph, however, gave the impression of *plotting revenge*, albeit against individuals who had not committed an offense against him. This made him extremely unpopular. Danny, on the other hand, reacted aggressively when he was *provoked* in some way. Though the provocation almost invariably seemed trivial, and his reaction indefensible, Danny's behavior was tolerated, as he took out his rage upon himself, or perhaps an inanimate object, leaving his bystanders bewildered but unscathed.

In the pathologically aggressive child, then, the presence of a revenge component has a significant effect upon the reactions and attitudes of persons in his environment, which in turn play a part in determining the course of his development. Danny's behavior was tolerated, while Ralph's was seen as malicious, engendering wishes for revenge in the children and the adults who dealt with him.

An encopretic boy

Charlie was five and a half years old when he was referred to a mental health center for treatment. He had begun soiling at the age of four, having been toilet-trained when he was two and a half years old, not without some struggles. Charlie was a charming, electric, bright youngster who impressed everyone in his orbit with his friendliness. Depressed patients in the waiting room often seemed lifted in spirit by Charlie's sparkle.

Charlie's mother, a stern and preoccupied single woman, was a student at a local university, and had assigned many of the tasks of Charlie's upbringing to her mother, who was a warm and indulgent caretaker. When the grandmother was for some reason unable to care for Charlie, he was 'passed on' to an aunt, who appeared to be extraordinarily impatient with the boyish capers and the symptoms of her nephew. She had made it quite clear that she had little tolerance for the soiling, whereas Charlie's mother and grandmother tried to view the encopresis as 'something that would go away'. It was upon the aunt's insistence that Charlie was brought to the clinic.

Charlie was seen twice-weekly by a female therapist, who found him quite engaging and was aware of a temptation to indulge the child, much in the manner of his grandmother. To her surprise, Charlie brought up the subject of the soiling, saying 'I'm here because I sometimes mess my pants.' Asked how he thought it happened, he answered, 'I do it because I want to.' Having made this clear, he would have nothing more to say on the subject.

The sessions soon began to involve some rather messy play, which was not to the therapist's taste, but which she felt to be a necessary ingredient in the path to the understanding of the messy symptom which had brought Charlie to treatment. On one occasion Charlie declared that one of the tables in the playroom was a stove, and importuned his therapist to join him in pouring water into a can, adding crayons and paper, and 'cooking' the mixture. He also managed to set up this scene close to the end of the session, so that it fell to his therapist to restore the playroom to rights after he had skipped off with the family member who had brought him for his appointment.

Upon recognizing that she was playing the part of the grandmother in the transference, the therapist felt obliged to set some limits on the playroom activity; and following this decision, she informed Charlie that he was to stop the watery play several minutes before the end of the session. Charlie balked, announcing, 'You're just like Aunt Clare!' Refusing to help restore the playroom to order, he stomped out of the room.

In the following session, Charlie acted out the symptom which had brought him to treatment. Early in the water play he asked the therapist to stand behind a chair and count to one hundred with her eyes closed. Charlie then removed the seat cushion from another chair and seated himself upon the webbing. At the count of fifty, he ordered: 'Stop counting!' As the therapist dutifully stopped, he exclaimed, 'Now! Do you smell anything?' He had positioned himself in such a way as to be able to move his bowels; and since he was wearing long trousers, he felt it necessary to call attention to what had happened.

The therapist managed to comment: 'I sure do smell something, Charlie. And I remember you told me you did it because you wanted to. Now, can you tell me why you wanted to mess your pants right now?'

'Sure,' he replied. 'To see what you would do.'

'But why now? Why not long before now?'

'Cause I knew you were going to make me clean up my mess like you did last week,' he said, squirming in his discomfort.

'So that's how you let me know you were mad at me,' said the therapist. 'You know, you could have just told me you were mad.'

Charlie began to cry. 'She never listens!' he said, sobbing.

'She?'

'Yes. Aunt Clare.'

It seemed, upon investigation, that the encopresis had become largely confined to those periods during which Charlie was in the care of his aunt, who resented his presence and who had a negative attitude toward children in general and toward Charlie in particular. There had been 'accidents' at home and with his grandmother, but with Aunt Clare he seemed to have proven his claim that he did it because he wanted to. In describing his aunt, Charlie said simply, 'She's so fernickity.' And of course, the very best way to get even with a fernickity aunt is to smear one's bottom and clothing with feces when in her care. It is the rare individual, in fact, who can be objective about this symptom: Anthony (1972) refers to the encopretic child as 'the agencies' most unpopular customer' (p.611), citing a rush of referrals when it became known that he was conducting a research project on the subject of fecal soiling. Charlie, a 'discontinuous' encopretic, or one who had regressed after having been toilet-trained, fits Richmond *et al.*'s description of these children as unusually obedient and conforming, seeming to 'control manifestations of hostility and aggressiveness, except for their soiling' (1954, p.398). Charlie, I should add, was unique in his ability to articulate the revenge motive and the selectivity in his choice of targets.

Any discussion of the treatment of the clinically or destructively aggressive child is likely to have a 'how to' flavor, as it clearly involves the modification of behavior. Anna Freud, however, states it elegantly when she writes:

> [When] the aggressive urges ... seek expression in life in the form of pure, unadulterated, independent destructiveness ... efforts to control these patho-logical states of infantile aggressiveness by force, and efforts, with all the means used in upbringing, to urge the child to control his destructiveness, are bound to fail. The appropriate therapy has to be directed to the neglected, defective side, i.e., the emotional libidinal development. (1949, p.42)

Revenge and the child who internalizes

In 'Analysis of a phobia in a five-year-old boy,' Freud (1955a, Vol. 10) offers an example of symptom formation in a young child, Little Hans, whom he describes as a 'cheerful, good-natured and lively little boy.' Little Hans' symptom – his phobia of horses – was determined by Freud to be the product of repressed anxiety related to Oedipal issues, in addition to the boy's jealousy of his younger sister. After describing a conversation between Hans and his father regarding lively fantasy material related to the child's anxieties, Freud asks: 'What can be the meaning of the boy's obstinate persistence in all this nonsense? Oh, no, it was no nonsense: it was parody, it was Hans' revenge upon his father' (p.70).

Hans' phobia was related to many filial issues, including the Oedipal conflicts. Revenge, however, was seen by Freud to have been an important ingredient in his symptom, as the boy's anxieties caused disruption and consternation in the family, and sufficient concern to have brought Hans' father to Freud for consultation regarding his lively young son. His account of little Hans' phobia provides an excellent example of the following statement from 'Mourning and melancholia':

> The patients usually still succeed, by the circuitous path of self-punishment, in taking revenge on the original object and in tormenting their loved one

through their illness, having resorted to it in order to avoid the need to express their hostility to him openly. (Freud 1959, Vol.14, p.251)

Rochlin (1973) sheds light on Hans' phobia and his view of himself as victim when he states: 'The aggression felt toward someone whom we value or who represents a value to us turns unconsciously against ourselves. We may become phobic, thus victimizing ourselves, and effectively prohibiting aggression toward others' (p.32). It is frequently the agreeable, cheerful, accommodating child who, like little Hans, presents with a symptom which utterly confounds his parents: an inexplicable phobia, encopresis, elective mutism, or an eating or sleeping disorder. Often it is the pediatrician or the teacher who suggests that the parent seek help from a psychotherapist. These disorders, however, demand attention so insistently that even the most uninitiated parent is likely to discover that the child is a candidate for intervention by a member of the mental health profession.

The question of revenge in the mild, polite child who refuses to eat, or the timid little girl who has not spoken a word in school, may at first glance seem absurd. This child does not hit back. He is generally obedient to his parents. However, he may have found the one way in which he can express his consuming anger: his rage at being smothered and deprived of autonomy, or at being expected to provide ingredients in his parents' lives which are inappropriate. He cannot voice his resentment in words for fear of being shamed or rejected. Unable to contain his feelings, and equally unable to communicate them in words, he has found, perhaps quite by accident, a way in which he can extract *focused attention to his person* which offers some relief from his anger and frustration. It is not unusual for someone to have unwittingly yet seriously offended a child in some way. Having neither the skills nor the environment necessary to make his needs known in a traditionally acceptable manner, the child has thus resorted to measures which wreak havoc in his environment and provide, at best, negative satisfaction to him. The attention may be supremely negative, or even frantic, as is often the response to eating disorders or elective mutism. If he is fortunate, however, his symptom serves as an instrument in introducing a third party – a mental health professional – in an attempt to find a resolution to the crisis which he has generated.

The young child may himself be quite unaware of the existence of a *target individual* in his quest for relief from his frustration and anger. He loves his parents, at least most of the time, and of course he depends upon them. His parents, furthermore, may care deeply about their child and be bewildered by his behavior. And so, how can we consider including the concept of *revenge* in exploring the dynamics of the child's symptoms?

The parents are baffled, while the therapist finds himself assigned the task, among others, of discovering the source of the patient's symptom. If the therapist suspects that there is a retaliatory factor in the behavior of the child who presents with selective mutism or an eating disorder, has he committed himself to a *witch hunt?* Or, phrased more delicately, the pursuit of a culprit?

I think not. A witch hunt implies that the witch is evil and must be punished; and punishment, or revenge, is of course not the goal of the therapeutic process. The goal is to better understand the working of the mind of the troubled child, whose motives may be a mystery even to him.

Laub and Auerhahn (1993) eloquently state one of the incentives for the therapist, when they write, regarding the children of Holocaust survivors, that there is 'a tendency in children of survivors to become mental health workers; they have an interest in secrets, and a need to decode them and help those who suffer from them' (p.296).

Aside from the conscious and unconscious motives of the therapist, the *value* of discovering the source of the child's discomfort and of his efforts to 'get even' is manifold, including the facts that:

1. The symptom becomes less mysterious. It is connected with unresolved issues which are of supreme importance to the child, but which have not been articulated by him, nor perhaps recognized by his caregivers.

2. The choice of symptom is in many instances related to issues in the relationship with the parent. The child who refuses food, for example, may be unconsciously assaulting the parent who has an obsession with proper food intake, even at the expense of his own comfort and pleasure.

3. When the symptom is seen as involving the parental or caretaker relationship, a direction is created for exploration with the parents.

4. Seeing the symptom as a statement of revenge lends a focus to the work. This thought was elucidated by a colleague, who advised: 'We have to know *where to sink our shaft.*'

The work with Martin will illustrate the above thoughts.

Martin, a boy who shredded his clothing

Like Charlie, Martin discovered the most effective way of expressing his resentment of his parents' policies: by creating a negative impression of himself. Martin's revenge was played out by way of his clothing. He punched holes in his shirts, slashed his boots and his belt, and unraveled his sweaters. Martin was the very bright only child of sophisticated, achieving parents who described themselves as 'old-fashioned people who were educated in boarding schools and don't know a great deal about raising children.' Martin, like James Joyce's Cranly, the 'child of exhausted loins' in Joyce's *A Portrait of the Artist as a Young Man* (1992, p.242), was methodically going about the business of exhausting his parents, who had felt that they were getting along reasonably with Martin until he began shredding his garments. His teacher, astonished to find him with slashes in his shirt sleeves, recommended that Martin and his parents consult a child therapist.

Martin enjoyed his sessions, in which he used a family of dolls to depict a household of fighting, screaming people who expressed their antagonism in a way quite foreign to that of his own environment, where voices were seldom raised. The aggression was diffuse, however, and Martin gave no hint as to the issues between the warring family members; and to his parents' dismay, he continued to ruin his clothing. Wherever he was, at home or at school, he would take a pencil or any sharp object which happened to be handy, pierce a hole in his pants or shirt and then proceed to rip the cloth from the cut threads. He made rags out of wool and corduroy. He clipped buttons and threw them away.

Eventually, after several trips to the boys' apparel shop with his fastidious, perplexed and indignant mother, Martin began to express himself more forthrightly in his therapy sessions. Putting aside the doll family, Martin chose pencil and paper and proceeded to draw a mother and father and their boy, who was standing behind a door. Scribbling excitedly, he began to describe rules and regulations about excursions away from the house. There were many forbidden areas, coupled with behaviors which were 'out of bounds.' Though the boy's friends were depicted as having no restrictions on their activity, the boy behind the door was held back by rules. When asked if the boy had complained about the rules, he answered 'No, not much. He didn't want to get in more trouble.' As he raged at the stick figures in his 'house,' there was increasing pressure in Martin's scribbling. Eventually he bore down with such intensity that the pencil cut through the paper. Close to tears, he exclaimed, 'They don't hardly want me to go outside my own yard! My friends can go anywhere they want to, and they think I'm a sissy. My parents just don't understand. All they want me to do is *look nice*!'

Following this literal breakthrough, for several sessions Martin continued the sequence of frenetic drawing, ending with furious slashing of the paper; and with this he almost simultaneously stopped destroying his clothing. Fortunately, his treatment was allowed to continue until he had worked through his frustration and feelings of helplessness about rather arbitrary and rigid rules. His parents, examining some of their practices and beliefs, were more than willing to negotiate with Martin on the matter of restrictions, concluding that 'he really knew where to push our buttons!' – an interesting figure of speech indeed.

It is worth noting that prior to the clothing crisis, *negotiation* had not been considered as a way of communicating by either Martin or his parents, who seemed to be caring and considerate but rather concrete, either/or persons. Martin was restless, frustrated, fearful of being excluded by his peers because of the restrictions imposed upon him, and did not protest verbally because as he said, he didn't want to get in 'any more trouble.' Actually, he was in trouble only because of his cloth-destroying protests! A perceptive child, he knew where to aim his arrows, and he did so because it had not occurred to him to *articulate* his resentment until the therapist picked up his clues. His parents, on the other hand, had not explored the motives behind his behavior; to them, destroying perfectly good clothing was simply incomprehensible.

His father referred to Martin's destructive behavior as 'a wake-up call.' This is an interesting characterization: the clothing shredding was *not simply a bid for attention, as he had always received more than abundant attention from his parents*. He was in fact getting back at them for their lack of understanding of his need for freedom. However, it would have been dangerous for Martin to have been more openly, physically aggressive in objecting to his restrictive parents, because, as Hartmann, Kris and Loewenstein point out, 'Aggression is dangerous…[when] it involves the individual in conflicts that are difficult if not impossible to solve, since they threaten the very object on whom man depends' (1947, p.21). Martin, furthermore, cannot be said to have *plotted his revenge;* he simply knew, at some level, wherein lay one of his parents' vulnerabilities – their overweening concern about their young son's appearance – and in his own way he brought about a compromise.

So it was in Freud's day, and so it remains today, the child whose parents are sensitive to his cries for help will seek the cause rather than punish the child while focusing upon the symptom. Little Hans' parents, being close associates of Freud, sought his help in determining the source of their son's phobia. In cases such as that of little Hans, and those of Charlie and Martin, there is parent cooperation, as well as a certain measure of sophistication and resourcefulness on the part of the parents. But these, of course, are the ideal circumstances for the child, his parents and his therapist.

A misleading symptom

There is seldom any doubt that aggressively biting another individual is an act of revenge. With children, however, the motive underlying the offense may require considerable exploration. A 'biter' may be a willful, combative child who seems primed for attack; or he may be an anxious, inhibited youngster who resorts to primitive oral aggression out of fear or panic.

Franklin had recently celebrated his fifth birthday when he came for his first appointment at my home office. He had been referred for treatment after having bitten one of his classmates at his suburban preschool. Franklin was the older of two sons of a young working couple; his brother, Sam, was two years old and was enrolled in a day care program. Franklin's parents were quite concerned that their son had reacted in such an uncouth manner to the provocations of his classmate, Sandy, though they had for some time felt uneasy on hearing Franklin's reports of teasing by Sandy, who was well known as the class bully. They were also aware of the fact that, as is true in many child development settings, in Franklin's preschool biting was considered a sufficiently serious offense to warrant stringent measures, including, eventually, dismissal.

In the initial interview, Franklin's parents described him as a timid child, with a vivid imagination and unaccountable phobias, such as a fear of fire engines. His brother, Sam, was more lively and aggressive, and had created considerable disruption in the family during his first year, as he had been a colicky baby who kept everyone awake, screaming throughout the night.

It did not require expert detective work to determine one of the underlying sources of Franklin's vengeance. In the first play therapy session, he drew a picture of his home, saying that *three* people lived in the house. This theme was soon repeated, in a drawing in which he tried to portray the mother and father and two children; try as he might, he was unable to fit the third person onto the paper. Though it was not explicit who was the superfluous child, it was clear that there was resentment and anxiety concerning his little brother. Perhaps Franklin saw Sam as the intruder; or, seeing his parents as overburdened, Franklin may have felt that *he* was now one too many. At any rate, Franklin left little doubt that there was a significant sibling factor in his retaliatory reactions.

Franklin was most creative in communicating his view of his family and his home. He spent one of his early sessions in arranging a puzzle-like toy in such a way as to portray a mother who built a moat around her house and gave many messages indicating that she enjoyed being alone. This graphic portrayal was followed by an arrangement depicting a father who invited children and dogs to romp around him. I seldom saw Franklin's mother, who brought him for his appointments; after the first few sessions she began the practice of dropping him off at the door, waving to him as he walked up the steps to my home office. On the other hand, his father, who picked him up at the end of the session, seemed quite engaged with his son, often reporting a few events of interest which had occurred during the preceding week.

Franklin's view of his parents was supported by some interesting interactions in the early stages of the therapy. The setting of the home office inevitably affects the transference and the possibilities of neutrality, while also contributing, ideally, to a sense of ease in the child's early adjustment to the new situation.

From the first play therapy session, Franklin exhibited curiosity, not directly about me, his therapist, but about my husband, who, although there was no visible evidence of his presence, inspired impressive curiosity in Franklin. Remarkably, he was able to perceive the opening and closing of the front door, two rooms away from the playroom, confirming his interest in being in touch with 'the man of the house.' Given his portrayals of his mother, it is understandable that he should consider his female therapist to be someone who would be less wholeheartedly connected with him and his interests and needs than her husband.

As Franklin began to select toys representing his interests, his symbolic play became increasingly aggressive. Choosing cowboys and Indians, he nevertheless manufactured scenes depicting maritime adventures and frightening episodes involving good guys, bad guys and sharks, which ate people. In these scenarios, his imagination and his tolerance for anxiety had their limits. When the scene reached a certain level of distress, he would leave the project, changing his direction.

Franklin began to hit his stride, therapeutically speaking, when he discovered a wooden ship in the office: a souvenir object which had been more or less hidden behind a large decorative plant. In his play with this ship, he depicted maritime crises in which people were thrown overboard and eaten by sharks. To protect the fragile sailing ship and to pursue an avenue which seemed potentially productive, I soon purchased a large plastic pirate ship to replace the wooden vessel. Since the pirates wielded knives, swords and guns, I put them aside, in order not to appear to encourage violence in the child.

Franklin, delighted by the introduction of this new medium for his play, quickly searched the ship before asking, with a frown, 'But where are the pirates? Where is Captain Ahab?' It seemed that he owned the very same toy, given him for his fourth birthday, and for a year had become immersed, with his father, in reading and acting out Herman Melville's *Moby Dick*, the selfsame tale that his therapist had for months been studying in depth in her own fascination with the topic of revenge. Franklin knew exactly what took place in each and every one of the eleven chapters of his children's version of the novel.

From the moment of the introduction of the *Pequod*, Moby Dick and Captain Ahab, for weeks the sessions with Franklin focused upon variations of the story of the Great White Whale. In this endeavor whales (the good guys) and sharks (the bad guys) were made from Play-Doh. Biting was rampant, with Moby Dick biting off Captain Ahab's leg and sharks biting at random. Often, as he played with the pirate ship, Franklin referred parenthetically to the story of *Pinocchio*, which he and his father read together, and in which Pinocchio finds himself inside a whale. He asked me to join him beneath the table on which the pirate ship stood, so that we might both be underwater. Near the table stood my piano, the pedals of which became sharks. Due, undoubtedly, to his father's attunement, Franklin was remarkably able in projecting the excitement and tension in his play.

Both oral aggression and revenge dominated the scene. And yet it was some time before I was able to determine the primary source of Franklin's resentment and the object of his retaliatory wishes. From his parents' reports and from his own comments he seemed genuinely fond of his little brother, whom in his drawings he had appeared to consider to be 'one too many.' Gradually it became clear that Franklin's symbolic expressions of aggression and hostility – the attacking sharks and other 'bad guys' – represented a very troubling ambivalence and resentment toward his remote and preoccupied mother.

A deeply caring parent, Franklin's mother had been seriously overburdened by the very disruptive year following little Sam's birth and his colicky nights, and had reacted by retreating into her 'moat-surrounded' persona, rendering her at times emotionally unavailable to Franklin, who during his first two years had enjoyed the pride and attention of both parents. It was learned through talks with his parents that Franklin, craving a return to his former status, reacted to his mother's distancing, distracted attitude by dogging her footsteps, talking continuously and generally making a nuisance of himself. The expectable and unfortunate result was that his mother responded by further retreating from his demands, thus intensifying the tension.

And yet it was not the mother-son conflict which had initiated the referral for psychotherapy, it was the fact that Franklin reacted to an affront on the part of a classmate by biting his arm. Franklin was of course getting even with Sandy, who had allegedly bitten first. A further look into the psychodynamics of his behavior, however, suggests that the rage expressed by Franklin was a displaced rage toward his mother, whom he saw as abandoning him emotionally upon the arrival of the small, disruptive interloper, the baby brother, Sam. Some resentment toward Sam was expressed initially in the therapy, when the little brother could not be included in the drawings. Soon thereafter, however, the primary source of his vengeful feelings became evident, as his mother was seen as unable or unwilling to offer solace to a miserable, replaced firstborn son. His thoughts were expressed in a statement: 'I'd like to be on an island, with just my Dad,' and in a dream in which the house was on fire, and the mother was the last to make her way out.

Franklin's parents were sensitive individuals who were not defensive in considering the sources of their son's difficulties. They were ready to make changes. Franklin was soon able to interact with the class bully and others without biting; and after some months of play therapy he set aside the shark – the bad guy – saying: 'The shark was *sorried*.' It should be added that the shark's parents were also sorried, as can be seen by the fact that Franklin and his mother, as well as his father, began to enjoy those occasions which are best known to working parents and their children as 'quality time'.

Misleading demeanors: Masked depression

In reviewing my records, I have been impressed and indeed somewhat disconcerted by some of the adjectives with which I have chosen to describe many of the angry, depressed children whom I have treated over the years. Marnie, a suicidal child who will be discussed later, was described as 'a bouncy child, whose sweet smile attracted everyone who came in contact with her.' Encopretic Charlie, described above, was 'a charming, electric, bright youngster who impressed everyone in his orbit with his friendliness.' Martin, who shredded his clothing, gave the impression of being 'sweet, somewhat seductive and apparently outgoing.' These children epitomized masked depression. It was not a recognition of their depressed affect which brought them to treatment, but their symptoms, which were disturbing to their parents and were seen by them as behavior problems.

Toolan (1974), in discussing masked depression and depressive equivalents in children and adolescents, says of the latency-age child:

> [He] displaces depressive feelings with behavioral disorders such as temper tantrums, disobedience, truancy, running away from home, accident-prone-ness, masochism (as indicated by the child who manages to get beaten up by other children), and self-destructive behavior. (p.144)

Adolescents, to be sure, have an even more varied menu of behaviors calling attention to the fact that they are in distress, and which are interpreted as anti-social acting out, masking their depression. Adolescents may resort to dropping out of school or exhibiting the many manifestations of delinquency.

In the context of the present writing, it may be crucial to determine not only the depressive component but also the retaliatory aspect of the child or adolescent's behavior, in order to understand the underlying reasons for his plea for help. Just whom is he attempting to punish as he punishes himself, failing in school, endangering his health or even his life, or infuriating his caregivers?

Adolescents' expressions of revenge

The therapist who works with adolescents is likely to find himself dealing with youngsters who have become vindictive and pathologically aggressive, or whose negative feelings have been repressed and who express their vengeance through symptoms. To begin by addressing the former, the vindictive adolescent is described by Lane (1995) in the following terms:

> When vengeance is a central organizing personality factor, the child has a harder time adjusting to the stresses and strains of adolescence, the deepening of existing problems, and the tasks that have to be mastered in the normally developing pubescent. It is the resurgence of pregenital drives that brings latency to a conclusion. But, in the pathologically vindictive child, often there

is a weak or absent latency, and the serenity and quiescence that accompanies this stage is missing. Frustration levels already low, immediate gratification demanded, the ego is easily overwhelmed by the adolescent's vindictive urges and grandiose fantasies... The result is exaggerated rebellion, opposition-alism and negativity, defiance of authority, acting out, and the avoidance at all costs of further narcissistic injuries. (pp.50–51)

School refusal: Darlene

While school *phobia* may derive from any number of factors – anxiety about a troubling situation in the home, difficulties in relationships at school or a conflict with the teacher – the element of revenge in *school refusal* is often not difficult to discern. Most frequently, in school refusal the child or adolescent is attempting to get even with a parent in a battle over control. Hersov (1960a) distinguishes be-tween truancy, or unlawful absence from school without the parents' knowledge or permission, and 'a refusal to go to school in the face of persuasion, recriminat-ion and punishment from parents, in addition to pressure from school authorities' (p.130).

At a workshop focusing on problems of school refusal and school phobia attended by mental health workers, educators and truant officers, the prevailing opinion was that the youngster who refuses school is getting even with an overcontrolling father, in a family in which the mother is relatively ineffectual and less invested in seeing that the child goes off to school. The child is usually demanding, and is often given to temper tantrums.

When the child makes a practice of not showing up for classes, the school personnel are likely to be quite as outraged as the parents, and perhaps more so. It is an insult to the educational profession; school refusal is seen as a manipulation which leaves the teacher, the counselor or the school social worker feeling help-less and angry at both the child and his parents. The child finds himself in a privileged position, one which he is reluctant to surrender.

Darlene, the 13-year-old daughter of a single mother, was referred for treatment by the school psychologist because of persistent non-attendance at a middle school. Her opening statement to the therapist was: 'I'm not going back to that school. I've given them one last chance.' The arrogance implicit in this pronouncement was felt keenly by the school faculty, many of whom had strong reactions toward both Darlene and her mother. 'They insist that I do my home-work,' she added. 'I want my mom to teach me at home, but she doesn't want to.'

Darlene's case is typical of situations of school refusal in that there was a significant element of collusion on the part of family members. Due to seriously irresponsible behavior on the part of her mother, until very recently Darlene had been cared for by her grandparents, who had indulged her in many ways, including acceding to her wish to attend a private school. Though she was pleased with the school, Darlene had begun to find her grandparents 'too old-fashioned' for her taste; suddenly she demanded that she live with her mother, an impulsive decision which was not questioned by her family. Finding herself responsible for her daughter for the first time, Darlene's mother was intimidated by the headstrong adolescent and set few limits on her behavior. 'I can't make her do what she doesn't want to do,' she said to Darlene's therapist, 'and I never liked school either.' Darlene was well aware of her mother's ambivalence and lack of authority; she was doubtless aware, moreover, of the fact that her wish to be home-taught by her mother was unrealistic. She may, indeed, have been contemptuous of her mother's very weakness, though this quality was a major factor in Darlene's history of victory in confrontations.

When her preferences were challenged by the school authorities, Darlene's first serious battle was set in motion, with negative transferences toward the 'bossy' school personnel; thus, she quickly set about reclaiming her presumed rights. Offended by their demands, *she would let them know who was boss.* Darlene might have been puzzled if it had been suggested that she was seeking revenge against the authorities; in her thinking, it was simply a matter of entitlement. Her rights had been interfered with, and 'they' would have to pay.

With this constellation of factors, it is imperative that the therapist's work includes family members. Adding to the difficulties of this work, however, is the inevitable fact that the therapist often meets with resistance on the part of both the adolescent and his family, thus finding himself strongly identifying with the school personnel, whose negative countertransferences toward the student and the parents are often expressed in markedly unsubtle terms. An adolescent's manner of getting even can be remarkably powerful and unsettling.

Anorexia nervosa

Hilde Bruch, perhaps the most widely known authority on the subject of eating disorders, stated of anorexia nervosa patients that many 'will confess that they had felt that by starving themselves they were hurting their parents, gaining satisfaction from the concern of others' (1977, p.296).

Although issues of retaliation or revenge are frequently less explicitly addressed in the literature on anorexia nervosa, there is often, as in other self-destructive patterns, a flavor of 'you'll be sorry' in the anorectic youngster's message to the parent, most frequently the adolescent girl's message to her mother. Characteristically, these are issues involving autonomy, with the daughter saying, in effect, 'There is one area in which you can't tell me what to do, or what to think, and that is my food intake. *You can't make me eat.*' This unspoken message, unfortunately, has a great deal in common with the unarticulated message of the suicidal adolescent; and indeed, in extreme cases of anorexia the patient is literally, and successfully, suicidal.

Masterson (1977) states that 'The principal problems [of the anorectic patient] revolve around fears of loss of self (engulfment) or loss of the object (abandonment), feelings of emptiness and struggles over autonomy' (p.477). He quotes Bruch's description of 'an unrelenting No' extending to every area of living: a rage expressed by opposition. (p.491)

The therapist of the anorexia nervosa patient is likely to find himself in the frustrating position of dealing with the opposition described by Bruch. As Burke and Cohler (1992) describe the therapist's experience, 'The anorectic's rage responses may resemble those of the borderline patient, despite the fact that her rage is only indirectly expressed through starving both herself and the therapist by withholding within the transference' (p.176). In the countertransference, they add, 'The therapist's discomfort in failing to cement an emotional tie may be experienced as quite active and aggressive ... patients may deny that they have any problem at all' (p.180). They describe the anorectic's mother's typically 'voracious intrusiveness,' to which the patient responds with firm, if pathetic resistance. In turn, the therapist experiences the passive-aggressive stance of the patient, with the resulting frustration and feelings of helplessness regarding the possibility of making an impact upon the patient's destructive behavior.

The therapist who works with children is no stranger to 'the unrelenting No.' I cannot begin to count the number of times the parent has said, in the intake interview, 'My child says "I'll go talk to that lady if I have to, but I'm not going to tell her anything!"' The child's resistance is a natural and protective defense, and even when there is no prodding on the part of the therapist it is often lowered spontaneously. The adolescent anorectic's intransigence, however, can be most unsettling. It reflects a deeply embedded determination, with visible consequences which are often shocking and in extreme cases evoke pity, aversion or even withdrawal.

The revenge component in the anorectic patient may be written in her appearance and in her very glance, but if her resistance is entrenched – if she is unwilling to express verbally her rage and vindictiveness to her therapist, and if she is dedicated to more destructive ways of communicating her dissent and inner turmoil – it may be necessary for the therapist, also, to pursue approaches other than the psychodynamic in his work.

Suicidal children and adolescents

In 'Mourning and Melancholia,' Freud states of the self-tormenting in melancholia that:

The patients usually still succeed, by the circuitous path of self-punishment, in taking revenge on the original object and in tormenting their loved one through their illness, having resorted to it in order to avoid the need to express their hostility to him openly. (1959, p.251)

Referring specifically to suicide, the ultimate self-punishment, Freud wrote:

Analysis has explained the enigma of suicide in the following way: probably no one finds the mental energy required to kill himself unless, in the first place, in doing so he is at the same time killing an object with whom he has identified himself, and, in the second place, is turning against himself a death-wish which had been directed against someone else. (1955a, p.162)

It does not require a leap of that imagination to translate this elegant formulation of the 'enigma of suicide' into a perspective on suicidal behavior in children and adolescents: suicide or attempted suicide in youngsters are indeed expressions of despair. In young children a suicidal act may signify a lack of understanding of the irreversibility of death. It may exemplify radical impulsiveness. With few exceptions, however, a major ingredient in suicidal behavior in children is a wish to 'make them sorry.'

Schrut (1964) sees the child's self-destructive behavior in terms of a need to arouse concern in a parental figure who has somehow given the child the message that he is a burden. Perhaps even more intolerable to the child is the belief that he is expendable. In these painful circumstances, he may have discovered, perhaps fortuitously, that 'a type of behavior which produced the most meaningful relationship with the most meaningful person in his life...had such a strong emotional appeal to the mother' that his behavior, however problematical, 'could arouse in her those reactions of concern which approach what the child really wanted from her' (p.1105).

A DISTURBING LETTER

In an article in the *Washington Post*, entitled 'Teen's suicide "the ultimate act of revenge against the world"', Peter Baker refers to the fact that 'the long suicide note, which singled out his parents in a hostile manner', was, for his parents, one of the most disturbing elements of the suicide of a teenage boy who drove his motorcycle full-speed into the wall of his school (May 4, 1990).

Suicide notes are a familiar feature of the self-destructive acts of teenagers who feel that they have not been heard by their parents or caretakers. A chilling example of the youngster's punishing cry for concern is seen in a letter written by an adolescent girl to her mother. The envelope carries the message 'To Mama, From:_____. Open as soon as you see it. Please open!' The message is as follows

Mama, I just want you to no that I am running away. I am running away because I don't think you love me any more. You never pay any attention to me, but I want you to no that I love you and daddy very much. I will probably never see you again because one of my friends gave me some kind of drug and he said if I take all of it that I will probably die of an overdose. I think that it would be best for everybody so I won't be in everybody's way. When you get my report-card I hope you are proud of me because I did the best that I could do. If I make the honor roll at least I have made you happy at least once in my life time. I hope you don't come look for me because my friends gave me over eight hundred dollars so that I could leave [town].

I am going to miss you a lot, bit I will probably be dead in about two days. After I get to where I am going I will write you a letter and then take my drugs so that I will be out of your life forever. Tell my friends, goodbye. There names are [she names seventeen friends] and all of my teachers and principle, and [five more names].

I had a good 15 years in this world but it is time for me to leave. Just remember that I love you and I always will. I have never made you proud of me so I hope that I will make the honor roll so that you will be proud of me. After you quit your job I thought about it for a long time and I no that you aren't going to have a lot of money so I thought it over so I no that you will be very happy now, because you won't have to spend as much money. I took some of my clothes with me so I won't be dirty when I kill myself. If you really and truly love me you don't look for me or call the police. Please just forget about me and never think about me just act like I was never born. I love everything that you have every gave me, I just wish that I was never born. Don't think you were a failure as a parent because you aren't. You are the best mother in this whole world, and daddy is the best father in this whole world, there is one thing I want you to no before I go, it is when I skipped school last year, my friends had some alcohol over there house and needles. I tried the alcohol but not the needles. That is one reason I am going to kill myself because I think I am hooked on alcohol. Some of my friends gave me a bottle of alcohol every two weeks and I would drink it down so fast. I am so sorry but when I see daddy drunk I say to myself I remember when you told me that I am just like him well I guest you were right. Well I am going to say bye-bye now. I love you and daddy with all my heart, and don't forget I am going to right you a letter when I get where I am going. Tell everybody that I said bye-bye and I love them very much. Love you and daddy with all my heart. I love you.

There is a lipstick print on the sealed envelope with the message, 'Sealed with a kiss.' The day after receiving the letter the adolescent's parents found her in a drug coma. She recovered, physically, and was placed in residential treatment.

The length of the above suicide note in itself attests to the anger and resentment of its young author. The repeated, almost parenthetical indictment, clothed as they are with statements of affection, convey the message: 'I insist that I love you with all my heart, even though you have made me feel like a burden in my dysfunctional home, though you neglect me emotionally and no longer love me.' This puts the responsibility for her past and future actions squarely on the shoulders of her parents. She showed them how she felt in the most dramatic way available to her.

A SUICIDAL SIX-YEAR-OLD GIRL

Shortly after her sixth birthday Marnie was referred to a mental health center, after having stated that she thought about jumping out of a window. Her father, Frank, had been in treatment for depression at the clinic for two years and took Marnie's announcement very seriously. According to Frank, her mother, Alice, was 'a shadowy figure in the family. She comes and goes and various relatives take care of Marnie.' When her mother was at home, however, Marnie seemed to be in more serious straits than when other relatives were in charge, as that was when she would act out her self-destructive tendencies. Frank reported that, while in her mother's care, Marnie climbed onto the roof of the apartment, that she tried to hitch-hike and was at one time found joining a group of adolescent boys who pressed her for kisses in return for candy and money.

A charming and expressive child, Marnie sought an emotional connection with her therapist, a female psychologist, almost immediately, saying 'I want to talk to you about my mother. I think about jumping out the window. She don't like me, she always moves to New York. When I want to ask her a question, she says, "Go to your room and play" in an angry way, like she doesn't love me.' In her early sessions Marnie seemed to be more aware of hurt feelings than of resentment toward her parents, though there were some subtle indications that she found some vengeful satisfaction in the fact that she was complaining about her mother and father, while they were paying the bill! Nonetheless, at some level she felt that both parents would be happy to be rid of her, that she could please them by being out of their way, and that they would regret their failure to meet her needs.

It was indeed fortuitous that Marnie's self-destructive thoughts were taken seriously, as she was quite successful in masking her depression in most environments. She managed to beguile everyone in the clinic waiting room with her sunny smile and her almost magnetic presence.

Had a statement such as Marnie's been made by a morose, complaining or disobedient child, it might have been dismissed by many parents and caretakers as simply a ploy, a bid for sympathy, as the phenomenon of childhood suicide is culturally unthinkable. In children under the age of fourteen, any death not caused by illness is often listed as accidental. It is difficult to acknowledge that young children, feeling unloved or burdensome, desperate, impulsive and lacking an understanding of the irreversibility of death, will perform hideous acts in an attempt to solve their conflicts.

Schrut (1964), in a study of suicidal children and adolescents, writes of 'Group 1' and 'Group 2' youngsters. The former were quiet, withdrawn, chronically depressed, schizoid children. Marnie clearly did not fall into this group, but would be characterized as one of Schrut's Group 2 children, who act out in a self-destructive way. These youngsters, having sensed a lack of maternal protection at an early age, develop a sense of unworthiness. Unable to reach the mother by being good, these children learn to arouse anxiety and guilt by their threatening behavior. Schrut believes that there is an unconscious pact between this child and the parent, whereby the child, unable to obtain unconditional love, finds a substitute: shock and concern over dangerous behavior. He terms this 'paradoxical suicidal behavior,' beneath which is 'the continual wish for maternal protection and help, which, in some suicidal adults as well as children, eventuates in "the cry for help" by a suicide attempt' (p.1107).

Marnie occasionally tested the therapist's commitment, or her measure of maternal protectiveness, by commenting, as she gazed out of the third story window in the office: 'It's an awfully long way to the ground, isn't it? And it would hurt if you jumped.' As the therapist spoke to Marnie about the likely finality of such an act, and the merits of talking about one's feelings rather than acting upon them, she experienced the impact of the threats conveyed by an accident-prone or self-destructive child first-hand.

Work with a suicidal child can indeed be extraordinarily unsettling. With a child of Marnie's age, the irreversible nature of death may be a notion which has not been assimilated, or which is doubted. After all, if angels are dead children who have gone to heaven, don't they also play around on greeting cards? On television, the hero who is killed on Tuesday may appear alive and well on Thursday. Cartoon characters tumble off cliffs onto their heads, and in the following reel they are charging off on their next adventure. Even if he has begun to grasp the concept of death as final, if he has reached an overwhelming state of desperation, the impulsive child may not consider the magnitude of the consequences of running out into traffic.

Aware of the young child's rationale, Marnie's therapist, feeling an inordinate and unwelcome responsibility for the near future of the child in her office, if not for the moment, said, 'If you jumped, Marnie, you could kill yourself. And if you did, you couldn't take it back. That's the end.' Further imploring her not to do something dangerous when she felt upset, she added, 'We can talk about it here, and between times, at home, you can kick the stool, or whatever you do when you're upset. But don't jump!'

Marnie's response was, 'They'd be sorry.'

The therapist, somewhat relieved that her young client had not said 'They will be sorry,' went on to talk to Marnie in as straightforward a manner as she could muster, hoping that respectful attention to the child's despair, combined with a certain logic concerning the consequences of jumping from windows, would be met with some consideration. The therapist was able to mask her own anxiety to the extent that she could 'talk turkey' with the child, respecting her sense of despair and encouraging her to verbalize her feelings of dismay, with the result that the sense of crisis gradually diminished. Though Marnie experienced some major disruptions during the following months, including temporary foster home placement, with the continued support of the clinic and her therapist, and with considerable work with her parents, she withstood the emotional trauma, and literally lived through it.

Countertransference in psychotherapy with suicidal children and adolescents

In discussing temperament I have mentioned 'the universal, if unacknowledged preference on the part of child and adolescent therapists … for the subdued, agreeable patient,' adding that the child need not be depressed, but that it is the repressive child rather than the vindictive youngster who is for many therapists the more welcome patient. We assume, of course, that the suicidal child is depressed; he may be quiet and withdrawn, or he may be openly hostile and delinquent (Schrut 1964, p.1104) but if he has made his suicidal ideation known, he is *ipso facto* threatening to adults who are concerned for his welfare. As Turgay (1989) points out, family members of the suicidal youngster experience pain, hurt, humiliation and guilt, leading to 'the wish to punish the attempter or take revenge by threatening to withdraw love and care.' (p.979) The therapist, too, may be seriously threatened by the angry impulsiveness of his young patient: suicidal youngsters have been known to attempt to act out their self-destructiveness in the presence of the therapist. The work with a suicidal youngster, or of course with a suicidal individual of any age, represents a daunting commitment, and one which may be met with little enthusiasm.

Furman (1984) vividly illustrates some of the trials of the therapist of the suicidal child, as she states:

> Suicidal youngsters often act out … exciting doing-and-being-done-to fantasies. They provoke attacks, insults, rejections and humiliations or they perceive and misconstrue the words and behavior of others in these terms even when the reality does not warrant it. Sometimes they exhibit their excitement by means of exaggerated or unrealistic tales of woe and usually succeed in involving their audience by evoking pity or guilt or anger at the presumed perpetrators of cruelty to the patient … Relationships with therapists tend to be drawn into all aspects of the hurting excitement. They are tortured and

humiliated as the patient makes them anxious and helpless. They are perceived as tormentors and forced to take active 'punitive' steps, and they are put into the position of the participating audience as patients reveal their excited distressing experiences or subject them to silent imperviousness. The patients who are most seriously driven to self-hurting and suicide may not share their difficulties or involve their therapists manifestly at all – the therapists are kept in the dark and receive their own sadistic punishment when they suddenly learn of the patients' suicides. (pp.252–253)

This is hardly an inviting description of the work with the suicidal youngster, and would indeed cause a therapist asked to accept a suicidal child or adolescent in treatment to hesitate. In discussing the suicidal adolescent, Bemporad and Gabel (1992) convey a similar cautionary message, in a somewhat less dramatic vein, as they state:

This propensity [to suicidal behavior] is understandably frightening to most therapists, and the prospect of a successful suicide by a patient who still has so much life ahead of him fills most therapists with a sense of dread, sadness, and personal failure…The suicidal adolescent represents a threat to the therapist's professional identity and to his sense of worth as a member of a helping profession. The range of reactions to such a profound threat can range from overprotection and grandiose rescue fantasies, in which the therapist believes that he is the one with sufficient ability to make the patient see that life is worth living, to the wish to be rid of such a disturbing patient and to blame the youngster for 'controlling' treatment with powerful suicide threats. (pp.125–126)

Even the 'grandiose rescue fantasies' would seem to provide limited satisfaction, as there is all too often a recklessness and impulsivity in these youngsters which precludes all but a temporary peace of mind in the individual who feels a responsibility for his welfare, and indeed for his very existence.

The question of forgiveness in child and adolescent therapy

In *Guilt and Children*, Estrada-Hollenbeck and Heatherton (1997) state:

The processes of forgiveness…have been almost entirely neglected by social Psychologists. Common sense suggests that guilt and prosocial behaviors, such as apology, play an important role in the forgiveness process. Perpetrators seek to be forgiven and sometimes victims wish to forgive as a means of dealing with guilt that arises from transgression. (p.225)

In the present writing, the concern is primarily with the victim rather than the perpetrator: the ability, or the wish on the part of the child to modify his search for revenge by forgiving his parent/caretaker. From a psychoanalytic perspective, the value of forgiving his parents for the child is perhaps best stated by Melanie Klein, (1975) as she writes

> If we have become able, deep in our unconscious minds, to clear our feelings to some extent towards our parents of grievances, and have forgiven them for the frustrations we had to bear, then we can be at peace with ourselves and are able to love others in the true sense of the word. (p.343)

In considering the question of forgiveness in child and adolescent therapy, we must first ask: At what developmental level is the process of forgiving a relevant issue? If we see forgiveness as a part of the healing process on the part of the wounded individual or, as I have stated in another context, as a part of the process of mourning the passing of revenge, when is it appropriate to think of children as agents of forgiveness?

First, a distinction should be made between pardoning and forgiving. I would suggest that pardoning involves the act of making a statement, the aim of which is to mitigate the consequences of a behavior or an attitude which is considered to be reprehensible or hurtful. By issuing a statement, President Ford pardoned former president Nixon. The fact that this act of pardon was met with considerable emotion, including anger and dismay, attests to the negative reaction to the introduction of an act of pardon on the part of those who have sought revenge and feel cheated by the fact that words can appear to cancel possibilities of retribution.

On the other hand, a child who has sought revenge may later decide, for many reasons, to pardon his perpetrator. He may be tired of the battle; he may sense that he stands to lose if the war should continue. Pardoning, in a sense, is a canceling of hostilities, and may be welcome on all fronts.

Forgiveness is another matter. Forgiveness involves a change in emotional attitude, and as such requires a maturity which is not crucial to the process of pardoning. Forgiveness is considered to be a mature response to an offense against the individual, as expressed in the Lord's Prayer: 'Forgive us our trespasses as we forgive those who trespass against us.' In considering the child's relationship to forgiveness, what can be considered to be a sin or a 'trespass' against the child? This question might be answered quickly and firmly by adults; but what does the child see as constituting a sin against him, or a crossing of boundaries?

To approach this question, we must first ask: What is the child's understanding of his rights? For his behaviour can only be seen either as seeking revenge or as offering forgiveness when he has developed the concept that he has been wronged. There is of course a vast difference between the toddler's and the adolescent's view of the parent as the rightful authority. Likewise, there are wide differences in personality which contribute to variations in children's perceptions of fairness in parental treatment. The very narcissistic youngster, feeling entitled to having his wishes fulfilled, will be slow to forgive his parent for not indulging him, while the anxious, diffident child: the child who internalizes and who has more modest expectations regarding his elders and his rights, might think in terms of being forgiven rather than forgiving.

Forgiveness, then, may not be an issue in the therapy with young children. Indeed, regardless of age, it is not inevitably a component in the work, though the patient may feel that he has been wronged by significant persons. It can, however, be a major concern of the child if he has been led to believe that to forgive is an obligation which, if not fulfilled, will bring about a sense of guilt. If the child feels obliged to forgive, he may say the required words, but they may be perfunctory echoes, or he may simply not comprehend what he is saying. Thus we must ask: At what age does forgiveness have meaning for the child?

Forgiveness and mourning

If, as suggested above, we liken the process of forgiveness to that of mourning, we may view forgiveness as an ongoing process, like that of relinquishing a cherished object or selfobject, a process which requires painstaking work. Assuming this analogy is valid, we must ask: At what age is the child capable of mourning?

In the Abstracts of the first twenty-five volumes of *The Psychoanalytic Study of the Child*, (1972) there are twenty-one references to mourning, and no references to forgiveness. If we think of forgiveness, however, in terms of decathecting, or relinquishing revenge, then it may be fruitful to consider its parallels with the process of mourning, by asking: 'At what age is the question of forgiveness relevant?'

There has been considerable controversy in the literature regarding the age at which the child has the capacity for mourning. Some of the more definitive articles on this subject are those of Bowlby and Wolfenstein. In 'Grief and Mourning in Infancy and Early Childhood', (1960) Bowlby challenges the statements of analysts, including Freud and Burlingham and Heinicke, that the child of less than two years old is not capable of mourning a lost object. Bowlby believes firmly in an essential similarity in the grief and mourning processes of adults and very young children, stating:

> My principal aim [in this article] will be to demonstrate that the responses to be observed in young children on the loss of the mother figure differ in no material respect (apart probably from certain consequences) from those observed in adults on loss of a loved object. (p.10)

This viewpoint has attracted considerable criticism: the reaction in itself attesting to the importance of the question of the young child's ability to experience a period of mourning. Anna Freud (1960) states that 'We [Freud and Burlingham] have hesitated...to apply the term mourning in its technical sense to the bereavement reactions of the infant'. (p. 58) These authors are of the opinion that the process of mourning in the child cannot be compared with that of the adult Spitz also takes exception to Bowlby's arguments stated above, saying that 'Bowlby…takes it for granted that the infant and the toddler both have a personality quite comparable to that of the grownup; both are therefore presumed to go through the same kind of mourning process as the adult when losing a love object' (1960, p.91).

Wolfenstein, in *How is Mourning Possible?* (1966) states that before adolescence the child is not capable of the painful and gradual decathexis necessary for mourning. He must either cling to the lost object or transfer his libidinal energy to another. Children, she believes, 'operate on an all-or-none basis' (p.110) and lack the capacity for a gradual 'dosage in emotional letting go.'

Bowlby (1980), contesting the view of Wolfenstein and others regarding the young child's capacity for mourning, states his conviction that 'There seem good grounds for attributing a germinal capacity for mourning to young children at least from sixteen months onwards.' (p.437) Of special interest in the context of this book is, however, Bowlby's statement that (regardless of the controversy concerning the age at which mourning is possible), 'There are good reasons for retaining the term mourning and using it to refer to all the psychological processes, conscious and unconscious, that are set in train by loss'. (p.18)

It would seem that the following question is central to the controversy regarding the age at which mourning, or forgiveness, is possible: At what stage of development has the child grown beyond the stage of operating, as Wolfenstein phrases it, 'on an all-or-none basis'? or when does he attain the 'capacity for gradualness … for this kind of dosage in emotional letting go?' Phrased in another way, Gartner (1992) has stated; 'Mature forgiveness is an integrated realistic view that contains both good and bad aspects of the self and others'. (p.23)

It should be noted that in asking 'at what stage is the child capable of forgiveness?' we are considering optimal, or at least normal, child development. If the child does not graduate from the 'all-or-none', or 'good-guy, bad-guy' stage, this presages the development of a borderline personality disorder. In this context, Hunter (1978) reaches the following conclusion regarding the capacity for forgiveness, in stating:

> The infant develops good, satisfying introjections and projections as well as the bad unpleasurable ones. It is in this balance, and in his early experiences of gratification, that the individual's capacity for belief in good objects and a good self originate. Certainly it has seemed to me during therapy that without an early relationship to what Winnicott called an 'ordinarily devoted' figure, plus a transference that recreates this, and a therapist that can sustain and work this through with the patient, accommodation to old and new injuries by way of forgiveness cannot be achieved. (p.170)

The writers cited above have considered the question of the child's ability to mourn a lost object: the parent or other caregiver (Bowlby (1980); Freud and Burlingham, Spitz (1960); Wolfenstein (1966)) and the capacity for forgiveness (Gartner (1992); Hunter (1978)). Both of these topics seem to address interconnected issues, for in discussing forgiveness, or the relinquishing of vengeance, we are considering the loss of a selfobject: the passage, as it were, of the energizing, satisfying pursuit of 'sweet' revenge. This, then, also involves mourning.

In considering 'to what extent is the young child capable of the gradual relinquishment of the pleasure of getting even?' some case material will provide a focus. A number of experiences in the practice of psychotherapy with latency children have led this writer to believe that, to some extent, young children are able to decathect, or work through their vengefulness through repetitive play. Two examples are taken from the work with Claude, a six-year-old boy, and Franklin, the boy who bit his classmate described earlier.

CLAUDE

Claude, an emotionally fragile child who was at the center of a bitter divorce struggle, was frequently found weeping at his desk in his first grade class. He avoided playground roughhouse games and clung to his teacher. It was sometimes difficult to understand his reluctantly spoken messages: I was gratified to learn that his parents had enrolled him in a school program of speech therapy.

For several weeks in play therapy, Claude's play centered upon a large toy truck built to transport many small cars and vans. He obsessively sorted them, named them and drew them. Claude was gifted artistically and was able to a certain extent to express himself through drawing; his human figures, interestingly, were tiny and squared-off, with expressionless faces.

Gradually Claude began to roll the small cars around on the playroom table, with an occasional 'accident'. The offending car was taken to court and fined. Once in a while a car would go out of control and intentionally ram another vehicle. As this activity escalated and Claude seemed to become more energized himself, there were shouts and threats. There was little doubt that Claude was lashing out, symbolically, at a perpetrator; yet the villain's identity was for some weeks unclear. It was not until he carried the frantic scene to the floor of the office that the plot began to unfold.

Claude placed all of the little cars on the floor, chose one sleek convertible which challenged all of the two dozen others and proceeded to smash the convertible into the back of cars and vans and pickup trucks, symbolically demolishing them. Inviting me to join him on the scene, my role was to collect the scattered victims and replace them.

For several weeks this scene was reenacted, comprising about the last fifteen minutes of the therapy session. The identities of the convertible and the others were never articulated; and I speculated, but did not ask, as some questions will effectively bring down the curtain. The pleasure of Claude's aggressive play was evident in his facial expression: his very color seemed to be enhanced as the little automobile sent the mob of cars flying. And then one day he seemed to have had enough of this enactment of revenge. Gathering the 'injured' vehicles and putting them back into the large truck he said 'Now they're sorry.'

'Sorry for?' I asked.

'They made fun of him,' he said, as though I should know. 'They called him 'Mumbo".' One would not expect a child of six to mention the fact that his classmates taunted him because of his frailties, including his speech impediment. It might be supposed that Claude somehow wagered that his therapist would 'catch on' to what he was trying to express, as he spent his energy tormenting the tiny metal vehicles. Once he had identified the defendant/convertible/'Mumbo', he was able to talk about his rage, frustration and humiliation and his need to strike out at the humiliating cars and pickup trucks, knowing at some level that he and his therapist were discussing his classroom anguish.

Gradually his fervent acting out decelerated: one might say that this relinquishing of the furious activity represented the decathexis of the lost object: the pleasure of the vengeful 'wrecking'. At the same time it was reported that he was becoming more assertive in his classroom and on the playground and gaining a new measure of respect from his classmates.

Claude brought closure to this phase in his treatment when he began the session one day with an unusually aggressive attack upon the assembled vehicles, then quickly returned them to their carrier truck, saying 'I feel like drawing.' He leafed through the tablet reserved for him, glancing at the pencilled figures, many of them ghoulish, then carefully selected some pastel crayons and proceeded to draw a stunning scene of the sun setting over the ocean.

Claude has never before nor since depicted serenity in this way. Nor has he since engaged in the frantic car-wrecking activity. He had clearly worked through an issue of revenge in his fantasy play. This process might be seen as similar to the mourning process, by which he decathected the rage, doing so in a piecemeal way. Wolfenstein considers the young child to be incapable of, or unready for, this process. Claude's accomplishment might be seen as working through. But can it be considered a process of forgiveness? That is debatable. He had apparently gained assertiveness to the extent that he had gained favor in his relationship with his peers. Whether or not his developmental step constituted forgiveness is another question, which for this writer remains unanswered.

FRANKLIN

In a very similar way, Franklin gradually relinquished the frantic oral aggression which so spectacularly characterized his play in the first weeks of his treatment. As he began to play out his rage at his little brother and his preschool classmates, his delight at the symbolic biting was remarkable to behold. Moby Dick and 'Monstro', the whale which swallowed Pinocchio, were his heroes; the pedals of the piano in the office/playroom became sharks' teeth; he went so far as to announce that he didn't want the day to come when he would begin losing his front teeth. (Landmarks of pride in maturing are not the same for all children!) As he gradually worked through some of his rage, however, his fixation on biting and swallowing began to give way to other interests. He began to set aside the pirate ship in favor of a doll-house with men, women, children, furniture and chairs to stimulate his imagination. When the ship became a 'good guy boat' and he began to name the 'people' after persons in his life, it was clear that he was beginning to put aside his rancor at his rival and the others who annoyed him in favor of addressing some other issues in his life.

For weeks Franklin began the session with the pirate ship and the sharks, almost as though to get a 'quick fix' of oral aggression and revenge, before going on to other pursuits in his play. In Wolfenstein's terms, he was only slowly willing to abandon the libidinal attachment to these symbols of his urge to bite. He did, however, relinquish his attachment to oral aggression, both in his play and in his relationships. Admittedly a very negative feedback influenced his relinquishment of biting at his preschool: the threat of expulsion. And yet, he also decathected the oral aggression in his play in the therapy setting, where judgments were not made regarding his choice of methods of communication.

Franklin gradually relinquished his expressions of revenge, laboring through the process in a way which was somewhat akin to the process of mourning. At the same time, he apparently began to have a more favorable opinion of his younger brother, the putative symbolic recipient of the fantasised bites. Again we would ask: Did he forgive those toward whom he had felt resentment and a longing for revenge? In his own way, it would seem that he did.

REVENGE AND FORGIVENESS AS SEEN BY SOME SIXTH GRADE STUDENTS

In the interest of exploring the attitudes of youngsters toward revenge and forgiveness, this writer requested a group of sixth grade students to answer the questions: 'What is the first thing that comes to mind when you hear the word "revenge"'? and 'What is the first thing that comes to mind when you hear the word "forgiveness"'?

Ninety-seven sixth graders from a public school in central Michigan participated. In order to encourage as much spontaneity in their responses as possible, they were asked to identify themselves only by age and gender. The respondents included 53 boys and 44 girls; 46 were 11 years of age, 48 were 12 and three were 13.

Although many of the responses revolved around the phrases 'getting back' and 'apologize', there were also many colorful accounts of the process of getting back and apologizing: accounts worthy of the exuberance of a sixth grader. Before these responses are quoted, however, I would like to offer some generalizations about the findings of this questionnaire.

The reactions of the youngsters seem to confirm the impression gleaned from experience, from literature and from clinical practice: that there is a certain discomfort, an uneasiness, or caution, in response to the subject of forgiveness, when compared with the emotional, sometimes volatile reaction to the word 'revenge'. The concept of forgiveness is abstract, non-specific, and carries with it the burden of obligation. It is interesting to note that it was often difficult to determine, when reading the sixth graders' responses, to whom they were referring when they wrote of forgiveness: the culprit or the forgiving one, indicating that the concept of forgiveness is not quite pertinent to their experience. It is a word, with certain associations, indeed, with an almost catechismic quality. When responding to the word 'revenge', however, the students seemed quickly to conjure up an association, if not an opinion, often with considerable gusto.

The word 'revenge' elicited expressions of both aggression and pleasure. Nine of the youngsters, both boys and girls, used the word 'kill'. Other responses included 'fight,' 'beat up,' 'kick,' 'hurt,' 'blood and guts,' 'murder,' 'evil comeback,' 'steamed up'. One twelve-year-old boy wrote, 'I think of power and I feel that I have the power to do whatever I want.' Another stated that 'When I have revenge I have ultimate power.' A few were more concrete: one boy wrote, 'Water balloon, toilet paper and squirt guns.' A girl's association was: 'Take their homework and rip it up.' Two eleven-year-old girls wrote, 'Fights, or jokes like mixing mouthwash and shampoo' and 'Ruining a pair of shoes.' Pleasure was implied in many of the responses and in two the joy in wreaking revenge was unequivocally proclaimed: a twelve-year-old boy stated: 'I love revenge,' while a thirteen-year-old girl wrote simply, 'Happiness'. It is interesting to note that none of the 97 girls and boys directed their putative revenge toward a parent or another authority figure. The only specified targets were siblings and rival gangs.

In responding to the word 'forgive', on the other hand, the majority of youngsters simply repeated the stimulus word or wrote 'to apologize,' suggesting a degree of discomfort with the word. More specific, concrete responses were: 'flowers,' 'flowers, candy, do their homework for them,' 'share feelings,' 'love, tender love, caring and kind,' and 'when you shoot a basketball and it hits someone on the head you say you're sorry.' An eleven-year-old girl wrote, 'Someone gives you an apology card.'

It is possible that the ease with which the sixth graders seemed to conjure up visions of revenge, as opposed to the apparent effort in responding to the word 'forgive', is partly due to the considerable amount of revenge encountered in viewing television. It is there, all around us, every day, for us to see and to excite us. On the screen, of course, there is little portrayal of forgiveness. Even so, is it not true that the content of television programs is determined, basically, by the preferences of the audiences? The twelve-year-old boy stated it succinctly when he wrote, 'I love revenge.' Forgiveness, in most circles, is praised; but forgiveness is not enticing. We consider forgiveness when we have to make a choice. Not so with revenge: we think about revenge when, as the sixth grader put it, we're 'steamed up.'

Countertransference issues in child and adolescent psychotherapy

I have already briefly discussed countertransference in the work with suicidal children and adolescents, and those with eating disorders. I would now like to address some of the countertransference issues which are likely to arise as an important facet in the relationship between therapist and patient in work with children and adolescents in general. Anthony (1986) states that 'Child analytic publications rarely mention the phenomenon (of countertransference), clearly regarding it, at all times, as a contaminant.' This is unfortunate, he states, as attention to countertransference 'stimulates insights in the analyst in parallel with his patient. There is no doubt that child psychoanalysis could make a significant contribution to this mutually evolving interplay of insights.' According to Anthony,

> The analyst may take the child as a transference object, or react to the child's transference to him as manifested erotically or aggressively; or he may identify with the child's parents and become overcontrolling or oversolicitous, or he may find incestuous fears and fantasies stirring as a result of direct body contact with the child. Such countertransferences are the daily bread-and-butter of the child analyst, and if he is as insightful about himself as he is about his patient, he will be alert to such reactions constantly, and at times even able to utilize them for a better understanding of the analytic process. (p.77)

Consistent with this thesis, Heimann (1950) has stated that 'The analyst's emotional response to his patient within the analytic situation represents one of the most important tools for his work. The analyst's countertransference is an instrument of research into the patient's unconscious,' adding that 'Often the emotions roused in him [the analyst], are much nearer to the heart of the matter than his reasoning.' (pp.81–82)

Because of the sometimes primitive nature of work with children, the therapist may tend to overlook the fact that his reactions to the child are countertransferential in nature. Is it not easier to say, of a child patient, 'I really look forward to my sessions with Scotty; it's a delight to hear him express himself,' or 'Next time I have to play Checkers with Daisy I'm going to put my foot down!' than it is to say of an adult, 'I find myself fighting sleep, listening to Mr. Jones,' or 'I want to look in the mirror before Miss Warner arrives?' With child patients, we may not feel constrained to think of our countertransference responses as 'instruments of research into the patient's unconscious,' in part because we tend to assume that anyone would react the way I do to that kid! But this assumption requires examination.

'GOODNESS OF FIT' BETWEEN THERAPIST AND CHILD

Thomas and Chess (1977) write of 'goodness of fit,' which results 'when the properties of the environment and its expectations and demands are in accord with the organism's own capacities, characteristics, and style of behaving'. (p. 11) Accordingly, poorness of fit is the result of excessive stress and dissonance between the child and environmental expectations. In formulating their research on temperament, they 'speculated that temperament was a significant variable and that healthy development depended to a major degree on a 'goodness of fit' between temperament and environment'. (p.29) This concept is also applicable to the relationship between patient and therapist, and most notably in the work with children and adolescents.

The staff representative of the therapeutic school who said, at the Open House, mentioned above, that the staff were looking for 'a few depressed children' indeed spoke of countertransference issues. By no means, however, must we assume that all therapists prefer to work with the subdued, depressed child. The angry, boisterous youngster may appeal to the therapist who welcomes a more pugilistic challenge. Fromm-Reichmann (1949) felt that as the therapist cannot expect to respond in an equally favorable way to all patients, he should determine the most favorable match between therapist and patient, and concentrate on seeing these patients. 'He should not feel he should be capable of treating persons suffering from any type of personality disorder,' she wrote. 'In the course of his psychiatric career ... the psychotherapist should learn what types of patients respond best to his personality as it colors his type of therapeutic approach.' (p.377) This caveat indeed holds true in the therapist's choice of child patients.

This writer's doctoral dissertation addressed the issue of 'goodness of fit' between therapist and patient, with the following question: In an urban clinic, where therapists were given the responsibility of choosing their clients, were there discernible personality characteristics which would distinguish between those therapists who chose to treat schizophrenics, and those who did not so choose? The research revealed that two qualities which were significant characteristics of the therapists of schizophrenics were flexibility and the willingness and ability to regress in the work (Durham 1978). And now, many years later, I find upon reflection that the therapist who chooses to work with children possesses in large measure those very same qualities: flexibility and the willingness to regress in the work!

Fromm-Reichmann's considered advice notwithstanding, in many clinics and in independent practices as well, the therapist does not always have the option of choosing the patients with whom he prefers to work, with the result that he meets with a wide variety of countertransference experiences, both positive and negative. That is to say, the fit may be less than ideal. In my experience, however, it is rare that a therapist, except for training purposes, is placed in the position of being required to work with children and adolescents. For those who find the challenges appealing, there is an unequaled satisfaction in engaging in child therapy but there are significant roadblocks as well.

We can assume that the adult patient has a motivation for seeking treatment – even though it might be to pacify a spouse, comply with a legal order or follow a cultural tradition, in most cases the patient has taken the initiative in establishing contact with the therapist. The adolescent, however, may be firmly resistant to the notion of psychotherapy, while the younger child often has little understanding as to the nature of his introduction to his prospective therapist and is relieved to find toys in the office and an authority figure who does not, generally speaking, wear a white coat. In effect, the therapist has to prove himself to be acceptable to his young patient, as well as to his or her parents. For most professionals, this is not a comfortable position to be in, and is one which adds a countertransference tension in the early stages of the treatment in child and adolescent therapy.

When there is a good match, the work, for the most part, will be exhilarating. When the therapist and the child are able to establish a bond and discover ways of communicating thoughts and feelings, a major hurdle is crossed, lending a zest to the work which is a powerful positive ingredient in the following phases of the treatment. Sharing the struggles and the joys of the child, developing an understanding of his or her idiosyncratic means of communicating, and watching his or her growth over time as symbolized by drawings, words and play can all elicit a positive countertransference which is unmatched in the work.

However, not all children are agreeable participants in the program decided upon for them and children are remarkably inventive in expressing their opinions about situations which are not of their choosing, or are in some ways threatening. The therapist may find himself dealing with hostile, disruptive behavior such as refusal to come out of a closet, spitting, kicking. The more subtly resistant child might insist upon filling the hour engaging in a silent game of Checkers for the hundredth time. In these situations, if the therapist hopes to remain sufficiently collected to maintain some psychological perspective, he will indeed do well to heed the advice: Physician, know thyself. In the work with children, it is important to maintain a certain emotional vigilance, as it is easy to lower the professional barriers and allow one's narcissism, fear, impulsivity, rage, pity or affection to take over the reins.

As Anastasopoulos and Tsiantis (1996) point out, it is important to try to delineate therapeutic boundaries in child therapy, as the therapist:

> Invariably becomes the embodiment of the trauma the child has suffered and of the deficit that the child has. Ruptures in the therapeutic process will inevitably be experienced by the patient as injurious. The patient's rage will be mobilized towards the therapist and may call for 'revenge', leading to acting-out reactions. (pp.15–16)

These authors take note of the therapist's responses to the child whom I have characterized as the child who internalizes, as well as his responses to the aggressive, vindictive youngster, also described above. In the work with the internalizing child, 'periods of silence or empty play are not unusual,' and 'sessions of this kind put a strain on the therapist, who may feel bored, frustrated, and useless.' On the other hand, 'the angry, domineering child may elicit retaliatory anger rather than firmness and gentle clarification of what is or is not permitted.' (p.16)

This retaliatory anger on the part of the therapist, the subject of Winnicott's classic article, 'Hate in the Countertransference', (1958) is not to be repressed, but must be acknowledged. Winnicott sees this anger as a crucial and necessary component in the treatment of the troubled aggressive child. 'It seems to me doubtful,' states Winnicott, 'whether a human child as he develops is capable of tolerating the full extent of his own hate in a sentimental environment. He needs hate to hate'. (p.202) 'In certain stages of certain analyses,' he believes, 'the analyst's hate is actually sought by the patient, and what is then needed is hate that is objective. If the patient seeks objective or justified hate he must be able to reach it, else he cannot feel he can reach objective love.' (p.199)

Countertransference and the parent–therapist relationship

The parent who brings his child for psychotherapy is likely to be anxious, bewildered and frustrated, at best. At the less sanguine end of the spectrum, he may be angry and resentful, perhaps feeling vengeful about the circumstances or the symptoms which have led to the referral. His attitude, be it hopeful, demanding, seductive, tearful or steely, will affect the therapist according to his own dynamics, that is his own unresolved issues concerning parent–child relationships.

Countertransference issues regarding the child's parents are complicated significantly by the matter of the professional/financial relationship between parent and therapist. For even as the child is dependent upon his parents, so the child's therapist, too, is dependent upon them for good will, support and trust; and it is all too easy for failures to occur in any of these areas. More frequently than is generally acknowledged, a child's treatment is precipitously terminated by an angry or envious parent whose borderline pathology was not recognized by the child's therapist before it was too late.

The parent of the child whom I would characterize as Exploited-Repressive: the child who tends to internalize his anxiety, will frequently tend to exploit the therapist as well. This is the parent who brings the child for an evaluation, requesting treatment and a recommendation for a change in school placement, only to disappear when the recommendation has been made.

The parent who 'runs errands' while his child is engaged with the therapist and fails to return on time; the parent who sits with his ear to the playroom door and asks, at the end of the session, 'Well, did you tell her how bad you were this week?' or the parent who pulls the child's hat over his eyes as he leaves, saying to the therapist, 'I hope you enjoyed it. You only have him an hour a week. You ought to know what he's really like!': these are the parents who try the child therapist's objectivity.

Although there is a large selection of books on the market aimed at the parents of children in therapy, there is little in the professional literature concerning the relationship between the parent and the child's therapist. Godfrind's in an article entitled 'The Influence of the Presence of Parents on the Countertransference of the Child Psychotherapist' (1996) focuses primarily upon parental interference. 'Every child therapist knows,' she states, 'about the pangs induced in therapist and child alike by parental intrusion.' Referring to the presence of the parent as a parameter likely to disrupt the therapist's functioning, she states:

> Interference from the existence of the parents is strongly in evidence from the planning stages of psychotherapeutic treatment. However, psychotherapy is only indicated for children if there is a parental collaboration and agreement. – This means that from the start of therapy the presence of the parents will weigh on the therapist's countertransference. The parents' conscious attitude – but, above all, their unconscious attitude – determines the possibility of bringing a child's treatment to a successful conclusion or at least to see it through a point dependent upon their tolerance. (p.101)

Unless there is clearly an extra-familial source responsible for, or contributing to, the child's difficulties, the parent will probably be defensive in his or her relationship with the child's therapist from the beginning. Many parents will expect the therapist to identify with the child (he is, after all, a child therapist). It is important that the therapist be as objective as possible in his communication with the parent from the very beginning.

CHAPTER 5

The Therapist's Encounters within the Legal System

In exploring the field of forensics as related to the mental health profession, I found a surprising ambiguity in the terminology. Under the heading of 'Forensic Psychiatry' or 'Forensic Psychology' in the reference system of a major medical library, for example, there were references to both *psychotherapeutic treatment of criminal offenders in prisons and/or mental hospitals* and *the practice of providing expert testimony in court cases.*

In the interests of clarity, I will use the term 'forensic psychotherapy' to refer to the work of the mental health professional who *provides treatment to the offender* in forensic cases, and the term 'forensic activities' to refer to the activities of the mental health professional who performs assessments and provides testimony, on the basis of which he serves as an expert witness.

Forensic aspects of the therapist's work

Forensic psychotherapy: Treatment of the mentally abnormal offender

'The essential subject' of forensic psychotherapy, in the words of van Marle (1997), 'is the mentally abnormal offender' (p.xi). The emphasis in this sub-specialty of the mental health profession is on 'the practice of psychiatry within the criminal and correctional areas. These would seem core, although not exclusive, activities of forensic psychiatry.'

O'Brien (1998) describes this area of therapy as 'a field of activity which was still defining its boundaries,' the main scope of which 'lies in the stages after verdict, that is, sentencing and subsequent care and treatment,' adding that 'few would disagree with ... [the] view that as a subspecialty, forensic psychiatry is now beginning to mature and to reassess its role and ethical position' (p.1).

Welldon and Van Velsen (1997) describe forensic psychotherapy as:

> a new discipline, being the offspring of forensic psychiatry and psycho-analytical psychotherapy. Its aim is the psychodynamic comprehension of the offender and his consequent treatment, regardless of the seriousness of the offence. It involves understanding the unconscious, as well as the conscious,

motivations of the criminal mind, and of particular offence behavior. It does not seek to condone the crime or to excuse the criminal. On the contrary, the object is to help the offender acknowledge responsibility for his acts and thereby to save both him and society from the perpetration of further crimes. One of the problems in achieving this object is that the offender attacks, through his actions, the outside world – society – which is immediately affected. Hence, concerns are rarely focused on the internal world of the offender. It is time to re-focus our concerns, at least in part. (p.13)

Working with the offender in the prison setting would seem an extraordinarily daunting task. The patient 'can stretch the therapists to their utmost with their impaired capacity to think and their tendency to act out in a destructive way. Via the transference and counter-transference a therapist can so easily be pushed into enactment' (Welldon and Van Velsen 1997, p.8). In this context, Cordess (1997) states that 'As a practicing forensic psychiatrist and psychotherapist, it seems that we cannot shrink from this, our central and crucial challenge: personality disorders in their various guises are our subject.' Referring to the clinician's role in release decisions regarding forensic patients, Miller et al. (1989) describe the very difficult task of the therapist who must 'continue to treat patients who are essentially "doing time"' (p.960). To make the task even more formidable, if the patient's release is for some reason postponed a therapeutic regression is likely to occur; the therapeutic alliance is thus negatively affected and 'to the extent that the staff feel more like jailers than therapists, they will behave less like therapists, and the hospital will be transformed into a prison' (p.961). 'Working with this type of patient can generate feelings of fear, hopelessness, helplessness, or even anger in the staff,' they state (p.962), adding that one strategy utilized in coping with the therapists' despair is to schedule regular 'me-times' on each unit, during which staff may air feelings about their tasks.

This work, indeed, is not for everyone. As in any profession, however, there are fortunately those who meet the challenges described above with an admirable resolution. In this context, it would seem apt to refer to some thoughts previously expressed, in chapter 2, regarding the therapist's countertransference in working with the Vindictive Character. In all likelihood, the 'mentally abnormal offender' will fit many of the descriptions of the Vindictive Character, including the diagnosis of borderline personality disorder. And notwithstanding the fact that the travesties of some offenders may render them beyond the empathic reach of the therapist, it should also be mentioned that 'there are therapists who greet this challenging (vindictive) individual with some measure of enthusiasm,' for many reasons, including an astonishment at and even an admiration of 'his patient's reckless aggressiveness' (Chapter 2, p.60). The incarcerated patient, of course, is paying for his recklessness. Nevertheless, his character, as well as his history, may be intriguing to the therapist whose life has been guided, or driven, by a certain measure of discipline and sacrifice. And most compelling is the fact that the rewards can be noteworthy. Forensic patients 'can ... make remarkable progress, if properly assessed with clear selection criteria and adequate treatment programmes that are implemented with the support and cooperation of the rest of the team' (Welldon and Van Velsen 1997, p.8).

In a study concerning recidivism – parole violation or reoffending in a correctional institution – Carney (1971) found that 'participation by prison inmates in a psychotherapy program was associated with a significant subsequent reduction in recidivism. It now seems clear that this reduction in recidivism was due, in part, to the decision to volunteer for therapy, i.e., the motivational factor, and, in part, to the impact of psychotherapy itself' (p.373).

In a refreshing philosophical article related to the application of community psychiatry in a correctional setting, Cumming and Soloway (1973) describe their experience as second-year psychiatric residents on a program in which they chose to act as psychiatric consultants in a jail. In spite of all of their discomfort and frustration, the fact that their 'philosophy of hope was dented,' and the fact that they began to fear retaliation on the part of the inmates when there were long delays in sentencing, they had some thoughts about how to make 'positive use' of their observations. They state:

> If one believes that jail represents the failure of a society, then those who are permitted to work there are either blessed or cursed with the opportunity to reflect on the impact that such failure has on the mental health of an individual as well as a community or nation. ... In our view, a prerequisite to good psychotherapy or to social progress is the belief that things can be better. Perhaps for the psychotherapist there is a slippery core of optimism in the idea that if feelings of alienation, fear, and anger can be talked about in the hostile world of the jail, they can be dealt with in the larger world outside the jail. (p.632)

A different view of forensic treatment is presented by Stanton Samenow (1984), who spent eight years as a research psychologist at St. Elizabeth's Hospital, a federal psychiatric facility in Washington, D.C.. With Samuel Yochelson, Samenow published a three-volume work, *The Criminal Personality* (1976; 1985; 1986), outlining a rehabilitation program based upon a study of the thinking patterns of the criminal rather than the outside forces which have influenced him. Although time-consuming, the program, which resembles a classroom rather than a psychotherapy group, has proven promising in changing ways of thinking about the criminal. According to his formulation regarding the criminal mind, Samenow would not view the criminal's behavior as *revenge against society*, but rather as *an exploitation of society*.

Samenow offers an interesting commentary on the challenges facing the mental health professional who chooses to work with criminals. 'When a person first begins working with criminals,' he states,

> he is likely to be in the position of a man who is expected to perform a cardiac bypass operation but has a degree in theology, not medicine. The criminal is quick to make mincemeat of such a well-intentioned but ill-equipped person. The greatest occupational hazard to people working with criminals is not physical attack. More serious is a rapid burnout of enthusiasm, commitment and interest. Mention the word 'burnout' to people in corrections, and they will solemnly nod. Increasing numbers of idealistic, genuinely concerned young Americans are entering corrections, eager to do a good job. Almost immediately, they confront a huge array of obstacles for which they are poorly prepared. (1984, pp.248–249)

Among the obstacles listed by Samenow are overwhelming caseloads, stacks of paperwork, lengthy meetings, apathy, cynicism and, occasionally, 'hostility from senior workers, who are battle weary from struggles with criminals and the bureaucracy' (1984, p.249). These challenges facing the forensic psychotherapist indeed support the statement that 'the work is not for everyone.' More basic, however, are some issues concerning his role in society: a role which he may at some point be called upon to defend.

The offender, the forensic psychotherapist's task and the offended community

Perhaps the best-known advocate for psychiatric treatment of the offender is D.W. Winnicott (1984), who spoke primarily on issues concerning delinquent children, but whose ideas apply to offenders of all ages. Winnicott acknowledged that due to the fact that 'crime produces public revenge feelings,' his position had met with very strong resentment in many quarters. He went on to state:

> My suggestion, one based on very definite premises, is that no offence can be committed without an addition being made to the general pool of unconscious public revenge feelings. It is one function of the law to protect the criminal against this same unconscious, and therefore, blind revenge. (1984, p.114)

Given a public sentiment of vengefulness toward the criminal, then, how will the forensic psychotherapist feel about his relationship with his client? It would seem that one cannot usefully consider the forensic psychotherapist's feelings about his work with the criminal population without considering *the nature of the crime committed by his client*. This will likely affect both his feelings toward his client and the community's attitude toward the criminal and the crime, which may in turn influence his own disposition toward the work with this individual. This question will be addressed by considering the public reaction to three highly publicized cases: those of Ezra Pound, tried for treason, John Hinckley, tried for the attempted assassination of President Ronald Reagan, and the sex offender whose rape and murder of a young girl, Megan, gave rise to Megan's Law. Society's and the therapist's work with delinquent children will be discussed later.

EZRA POUND

Ezra Pound, charged with treason during World War II, having broadcast, by shortwave from Rome, diatribes against the United States, spent twelve years in St. Elizabeth's Hospital after having been judged by psychiatric examination to be mentally deranged and incompetent to stand trial. According to E. Fuller Torrey (1984), a psychiatrist who was at that time on the staff at St. Elizabeth's, 'It is... significant that there is not a single mention of treatment for Ezra Pound in his entire hospital record' (p.252). Nonetheless, it is interesting to speculate on how it might have felt to have been Pound's therapist during those twelve years.

Coming from an extraordinarily talented, colorful and controversial individual, Pound's insanity plea was one of the most sensational in history. To add to the outrage caused by the judgment, he was given unusual privileges at St. Elizabeth's, causing further public clamor. Stock (1970) writes that during his hospitalization 'there was plenty to keep his mind active, including hostility in some newspapers, controversy over his work and his legal position... When he was awarded the Bollingen Prize for poetry, a new storm broke' (pp.423–426). Pound was known and highly praised as a literary entrepreneur for young writers, but even those in his coterie of students and admirers found him difficult. William Carlos Williams stated in a letter: 'He is just the man for me. But not one person in a thousand likes him and a great many people detest him, and why? Because he is so damned full of conceits and affectation' (Kapp 1968, p.416).

Judging by the characterizations of Pound, it is doubtful that he would have agreed to accept the services of a psychotherapist. According to Kapp (1968), he 'had no truck with psychoanalysis' (p.418). He is not likely to have placed himself in the position of being influenced by another individual. If he had agreed to meet with a therapist, however, it is interesting to speculate on how the experience might have felt from the point of view of the forensic psychotherapist. First, it would have been exciting, given the spotlight under which the patient lived. Second, judging from the public reaction to the patient and his activities, there would have been a decided antagonism on the part of society toward psychiatric treatment.

Given these factors, it seems that the reaction of the therapist who found himself in the position of offering treatment to Pound would depend upon his tolerance of the arrogance which is evident in depictions of the famed character, his willingness to be challenged by society's reaction to his client and his readiness to enter the fray, and perhaps his enjoyment of the challenge of working with a highly publicized figure whom 'not one person in a thousand likes.'

JOHN W. HINCKLEY, JR.

Ezra Pound was perceived as talented, creative and capable of attracting a following in any environment, including St. Elizabeth's Hospital. His crime, treason, one of the most egregious offenses, and the highly debatable insanity defense combined to make him a controversial figure, but as William Carlos Williams suggested, one either loved him or hated him. It is difficult to think of John Hinckley, Jr. in the same terms. Following his attempted assassination of President Ronald Reagan, and the verdict of not guilty because of insanity, the public was outraged. In *Breaking Points*, written by Hinckley's parents with Elizabeth Sherrill (1985), the shock and indignation of the citizenship regarding the verdict was not minimized. The agonized parents confirmed the fact that 'the jury was mercilessly attacked' (p.341), and that there were public clamors to have the insanity defense abolished. As Caplan (1984) stated:

> After disbelief, bewilderment, and wonder, outrage followed closely in the wake of the verdict. The American people saw John Hinckley shoot Ronald Reagan and three others over and over again on television, and reports of James Brady's courageous efforts to regain his health did little to quiet the urge for vengeance. If Hinckley had been lynched soon after the shooting it would probably have caused no more anguish to society than his acquittal. (p.116)

Like Pound, at St. Elizabeth's Hospital Hinckley made many requests for special privileges: notably, permission to spend time in Washington, D.C. unaccompanied, without any restrictions on his movements (Clarke 1990, p.63), thus further antagonizing the public. As as result of these and other administrative issues, some embarrassing and all highly publicized, John Hinckley's image has been one of the most despised in the criminal history of his country. Thus, with this aura, it would seem that to be identified as the forensic psychotherapist in a case such as Hinckley's would be a challenge without precedent.

THE INTRODUCTION OF MEGAN'S LAW

The public scorn for Hinckley, however, pales when compared with the outrage concerning the sex offender who abducts, abuses and murders; and the outcry is of course most vociferous when the victim is a child. The 1994 rape and murder of seven-year-old Megan Kanka by a man living across the street – a man twice convicted for sexual offenses – led to the passage, in 1996, of Megan's Law, which required the state to notify communities when a sex offender moves in. Although there has been controversy regarding this law, related to the offender's right to privacy, by the end of 1996 all but two jurisdictions required sex offenders to register with the authorities.

A *Washington Post* article regarding Megan's Law and similar legislation that followed (Russakoff 1998) quotes the parents of a young woman who suffered the same fate as Megan as saying that 'better inmate counseling and training are as necessary as tougher sentences' (Section A, p.10). Considering their horror and grief this is a remarkably objective statement, and does not reflect the view of the general public. According to Hyde (1997), 'Some people believe that money should not be wasted on attempts to treat or rehabilitate sex offenders' (p.35). She adds that, in fact, prisoners can refuse treatment before their release from prison.

THE FORENSIC PSYCHOTHERAPIST'S CHALLENGES

How, then, if he undertakes to work with an individual such as those described above, does the forensic psychotherapist deal with his feelings about his client? To what extent is he influenced by the nature of the crime committed by his client and the community's reaction to the crime and the criminal, often including a thirst for revenge? In certain respects, the pressures under which he works with the incarcerated client are unique. His outpatient clients, however trying they may be – whether they be chronic whiners, arrogant borderline individuals, anorectic adolescents or pouty children intent on getting their way – have not aroused the indignation of the larger society. When they leave his office, the therapist will not be reminded of their travesties by reading the newspaper or turning on the television.

When we consider the ways in which the therapist is affected by his forensic patient, it must first be remembered that the function of the forensic psycho-therapist *is not that of representing his client.* According to the definitions proposed in this writing, he is not an expert witness, and is not charged with defending the criminal, although he may later deem it appropriate to take the position of advocate when there is a question of his client qualifying for release. Until such time, though, the therapist's province is *the care and treatment of the criminal after the verdict and sentencing.*

To the extent, therefore, that the forensic psychotherapist is able to separate his feelings toward his client from the influence of public opinion, he will be able to minimize any prejudice in his work with the criminal who has outraged his fellow men. And yet there are intrinsic features of such work which lend it an under-standably negative ambience. Not the least of these, of course, is the potential for physical violence: violence which not infrequently may be directed toward the therapist himself, and which may imply first-hand revenge. Another frequently mentioned aspect of the work, less threatening but nevertheless enraging, is the patient's characteristic 'chameleon-like quality', with which he tends to manipulate and 'con' the therapist (Weiss 1998, p.173).

And yet as Weiss points out, 'The literature regarding working with criminals has downplayed positive emotions, including envy, admiration and titillation'. Weiss states that:

> Feeling attracted to psychopathic behavior can be deeply unnerving for the therapist. It is, I believe, easier to accept and admit to disgust and aversion, or the sense of being manipulated and deceived, than to admit to the glorification of a convict's sexuality or to the idealization of his defiance of authority. (p.174)

A colleague whose practice includes psychotherapy with incarcerated criminals described the 'morbid curiosity' and the 'fascination factor' which makes the work intriguing and in fact compelling to some of his fellow practitioners. 'Some of the staff,' he said, 'find themselves pulled into seeking out murder movies and horrifying TV programs which they wouldn't previously have thought of spending time watching.'

A most positive comment regarding forensic psychotherapy was made by Weiss, who states: 'As much as one might wish to decry the inhumanity of criminal behavior, coming in contact with the criminal more often forces the realization of their humanness' (1998, p.175).

The juvenile offender

Winnicott (1984) stated that 'At the present time the tendency is to do the best for the delinquent or antisocial boy or girl rather than to avenge. Except in the case of really serious crime the adolescent and young adult also come into this category' (p.203). In the decade of which Winnicott speaks, this writer worked with children in a residential treatment center, with a variety of youngsters, including juvenile offenders. Winnicott's statement brings to mind the treatment of a six-year-old boy who had set fire to the home of his foster parents. There was no question – no articulated question, at any rate – that this child was in need of treatment rather than punishment. Because he was an appealing, engaging youngster, his offense was seen as a symptom rather than as an affront to society.

Except in cases of extremely egregious behavior, the instinct of the psychotherapeutic community and the community at large, it is believed, is to look toward the child's future and to work toward healing his wounds.

Other forensic activities: The expert witness

The expert witness has for decades been a familiar sight for television viewers, both in fantasy and in reality. For years we have watched the triumphs and the perils of the witnesses in the *Perry Mason* series, and recently it was the rare individual who did not become riveted upon the testimony in the O. J. Simpson case. Whether or not the therapist identifies with the expert witnesses in these court scenes, it is clear that the witness's position is one of both power and risk.

In the criminal justice system, less dramatic, generally speaking, but equally subject to controversy is the clinician's role in court cases involving competence to stand trial, when there is an insanity defense or when there is a question of the defendant's release from an institution for the criminally insane.

Cook (1996), who states that 'Forensic child and adolescent psychiatry is not for everyone' (p.23), would seem to be making a generalized statement, as he offers the following caveat regarding the therapist's position as an expert witness:

> A physician considering entering a case as an expert witness should be aware that the forum is adversarial, involving conflicting legal and clinical themes. If the case goes to trial, it is quite likely that there will be an equal expert with an opposite opinion on the other side. A physician who does not wish to deal with the resulting questioning may prefer not to become involved with forensic psychiatry. (pp.21–22)

David Bazelon, a renowned judge and Honorary Fellow of the American Psychiatric Association, in speaking of the mental health professional's feelings toward forensic work, states: 'Persuading the psychiatrist to learn to love the adversary process of the courts is like persuading the old Tories to appreciate self-determination. Yet I firmly believe psychiatry's aversion to the legal process to be in large part the result of misunderstanding of the nature and goals of that process' (1978, p.144).

Herman (1990), in elucidating the potential tribulations of the expert witness, asks, 'Why would any physician complicate life with a liaison with the legal profession?' He states that:

> Forensic psychiatrists are often subjected to personal threats by unhappy, dissatisfied litigants. Custody disputes in particular arouse intense passions in parents, and a court-appointed psychiatrist opining for one parent and seemingly against another may receive frightening telephone calls at home, may be slandered, or may even be physically assaulted. (p.955)

Dietz (1996) enumerates some of the moral conflicts faced by even the best-intentioned clinician when he is asked to serve as an expert witness. The 'influences, distractions, temptations, hazards, and barriers in…[his] path include what a senior colleague might think, or in a high-profile case, the possibility of 'the attention of a new audience of potential clients' (pp.154–155).

Schetky and Guyer (1990), in discussing the evaluation of children and their families for purposes of civil litigation, state that this 'can be very gratifying work,' as, among other reasons, 'these cases are intellectually stimulating as one is able to observe, firsthand, the unfolding of psychological defenses, both healthy and pathological, that enable the child to cope with trauma' (p.968). In a more cynical vein, Schetky and Colbach (1982), in discussing both the positive and the negative features of the position of expert witness, portray psychiatrists as persons prone to 'retreat from the legal arena,' as 'many psychiatrists seem to prefer the company of their own appreciative patients, who do not challenge their authority quite so blatantly' (p.115). On the other hand, they note that the mental health professional may agree to testify 'for economic necessity, and various ego factors,' such as an exhibitionistic need for recognition: 'a desire to be in the limelight' (p.115).

Whatever the therapist's feelings about engaging in forensic activities, if he agrees to testify in court, he will run a greater risk of encountering unmitigated revenge, than he does in any other aspect of his profession. As Schetky and Colbach point out, 'Often what is said will clearly upset someone in the court-room... Delivery of damaging testimony...brings with it fears of upsetting people, with resultant retaliation. This is especially so in litigation involving paranoid individuals' (1982, pp.119–120).

An interesting account of a professional's quandary about testifying in court is an article entitled 'The reluctant retained witness: Alleged sexual misconduct in the doctor/patient relationship,' written by a bioethicist (Yarborough 1997). The author describes his many misgivings concerning requests to testify on behalf of defendants. The issues addressed included:

> the prospect of generating adverse publicity for oneself and one's institution, avoiding bias, giving testimony that is at odds with testimony given by colleagues, potential conflicts of interest introduced by reimbursement, the need of those who hear the testimony of bioethicists to appreciate the nature of moral expertise, the difficulty of assessing the quality of legal evidence which emerges from adversarial legal proceedings, and the need to consider what weight should be assigned to expert ethics testimony. (p.345)

This author is exceptionally forthcoming and unassuming (he was reluctant to be associated with the word 'expert'). He states, 'I agonized over whether or not money was clouding my judgment...I was troubled by the fact that I was being paid to say something' (p.351). The very writing has a ruminating quality, itself attesting to the moral quandary of this author, whose ethical scrupulousness is a credit to his profession.

On the other hand, there are those who, far from being intimidated by the potential threats inherent in the practice of forensic activities, relish the challenge. Ednie (1996), in discussing the challenges for women in forensic psychiatry, lists the traits of aggression, autonomy and assertiveness thought necessary for success medicine, law and the criminal justice system. These attributes could be considered attractions inherent in the subspecialty in itself. Forensic psychiatry, she states,

> presents a stimulating intellectual climate... It allows an application of clinical skills to complex legal problems. With society's increasing preoccupation with the legal system, it gives one a chance to be where the action is... It is an area of medicine yet untouched by the financial regulations that are impacting on other services. Coupled with the intellectual challenge is the chance for independent practice. Flexibility and freedom are two of the positive features of forensic practice. (pp.43–44)

The dual role of clinician and advocate

It is not uncommon to hear a therapist state that he had 'stumbled into' the business of testifying on behalf of his client, or that he 'felt that he should' go to court, despite his lack of experience in legal procedures. Driven by loyalty to his client, he has agreed to testify when custody issues were involved, or when his distraught client had been apprehended while yielding to the impulse to slip a bottle of perfume into her shopping bag.

Sleek (1998) quotes Steven Sparta, a forensic psychologist, as stating that 'Frequently, when psychologists are pulled into these cases, they're given tasks that are extraordinarily complex' (p.24). Sparta's term 'pulled in' is exceedingly apt, as it gives flavor to the fact that the therapist may find himself inside the circle of retaliation, faced with a task which is complex indeed. In testifying *on behalf of* his client, he is testifying *against* his client's adversary, leaving himself open to retaliation. Stromberg and Dellinger, writing in *The Psychologist's Legal Update* (1993), state this succinctly in the statement that 'With growing frequency, persons who are angry with the performance of the other side's factual or expert witnesses in nasty litigation seek damages or disciplinary action against them. This seems particularly common in divorce/custody cases' (p.13).

Strasburger, Gutheil and Brodsky (1997) address this issue in an article entitled 'On wearing two hats: Role conflict in serving as both psychotherapist and expert witness.' They state,

> In essence treatment in psychotherapy is brought about through an empathic relationship that has no place in, and is unlikely to survive, the questioning and public reporting of a forensic evaluation. To assume either role in a particular case is to compromise one's capacity to fulfill the other... Although

circumstances may make the assumption of the dual role necessary and/or unavoidable, the problems that surround this practice argue for its avoidance whenever possible. (p.449)

Appelbaum (1997) suggests an optimal response on the part of the therapist when requested by his client to testify on his behalf:

> Patients should be told why such behavior threatens to undermine ongoing treatment. An offer can be made to help identify another clinician to perform the forensic evaluation. In essence, the psychiatrist is saying, 'Your treatment is so important to me that I don't want anything else to get in its way'. If framed properly, this response can have a powerful, positive effect on the psychiatrist-patient relationship. (p.446)

Malpractice suits: The therapist as defendant

However conscientious he may be, however scrupulous and dedicated to his profession, by the very nature of his work the therapist may find himself the defendant in a malpractice suit. This is particularly true of the therapist who works with patients whose diagnoses include borderline personality disorders or psychoses. Among the claims frequently brought against the therapist are misdiagnosis, physical contact or sexual relations with patients, abandonment, improper release of hospitalized patients and implanting false memories.

However the plaintiff may formulate his reasons for adjudication in a malpractice suit ('I feel it's only fair to clear the record,' etc.), the element of revenge is indeed a major factor, if a paradoxical one, in the decision to *press charges against* the individual who has been engaged to help the patient.

Out of the large array of malpractice issues in the mental health profession, I have chosen to discuss those of implanted memories and sexual misconduct. These issues, with their titillating quality, receive lively attention in the press, whereas claims of misdiagnosis or 'practicing outside of one's area of competence' do not stir the interest of the reader or viewer in the same manner. Referring to the 'very considerable attention in North America' given to sexual misconduct between mental health professionals and their patients, Courtois and Weisstub (1996) state:

> It is difficult to ascertain whether this is attributable to an escalation of incidents or, rather, due to a heightened awareness among the population, given the movement of consumerism, and also due to the rise of feminist groups, or whether there is simply an inclination on the part of the media to report and confront the phenomenon. (p.183)

Litigation involving 'false memories' and sexual misconduct thus tend to lend an aura to the profession which needs to be counterbalanced by a less media-derived perspective. Courtois (1997a) cites the fact that the models of treatment of adults who reported a history of sexual abuse have been 'buffeted by a number of societal events and issues. Foremost among them: the widespread publicity accorded the new research findings on abuse and other forms of family dysfunction during the 1980s in the print media and in radio and TV reporting (and the "tabloidization" of abuse in some cases)' (p.465).

Alleged therapist-induced conditions concerning memory

Dissociation differs from repression in that the process of dissociation, as it is encountered in Dissociative Identity Disorder (formerly Multiple Personality Disorder), involves, according to DSM IV (1994), 'The presence of two or more distinct identities of personality states, each with its own relatively enduring pattern of perceiving, relating to, and thinking about the environment and self' (p.230). According to Brenneis (1996):

> Dissociation, as a state and as a process, is thought to play a pivotal role in traumatic memory. Current theories of traumatic memory … suggest that experience which, under less overwhelming stress, might be accessible to volitional recall by the dominant state of consciousness is dissociated and now dependent upon the evocation of the same state of consciousness for its retrieval. Thus, some traumatic memories appear only in altered states of consciousness such as in repetitive dreams, flashbacks, and stereotyped behavior. (p.1169)

Characterizing patients prone to dissociation as a defense, Brenneis states that these individuals also tend to be 'fantasy prone' or 'hypnotic virtuosos' (p.1172), and show a 'remarkable openness to influence and suggestion.' They are open to extraordinary ideas, and 'uncritical thinking is induced as much by facilitating instructions (such as to relax and let one's thoughts flow) as by inherent cognitive propensities. Still, a parallel between these facilitating conditions and analytic procedure cannot be ignored' (p.1173). 'Consequently,' he goes on the say, 'some concern may be raised that not only may fantasy prone people be likely to mimic dissociative processes, but also they may be fully capable, without awareness, of identifying an analyst's unspoken inclination to regard such dissociative expressions as potentially based in hidden trauma' (p.1174).

The above statements are indicative of the fact that the therapist who treats patients diagnosed with Dissociative Identity Disorder (DID) may find himself in an embattled position regarding his practices and his beliefs.

One the most outspoken professionals in the controversy regarding the role of dissociation in Multiple Personality Disorder (MPD) is McHugh (1995), who characterizes the disorder as a 'therapist-induced artifact' in 'distressed people who are looking for help' (p.959). In response, Putnam (1995) states that the charge that MPD is 'iatrogenic disorder produced in patients by their psychiatrists...alleges therapeutic misconduct of the gravest nature' (p.960).

In a 1998 article in the *New Yorker,* 'The politics of hysteria' (6 April 1998, pp.64–79), Acocella portrays psychotherapists who treat MPD in an extremely negative light, characterizing it as typical of 'mental disorders [which] go in and out of vogue' (p.72), and its therapists as exploiting their patients by encouraging the retrieval of memories of childhood abuse. The author cites a number of successful lawsuits filed against therapists by their MPD patients' alleged abusers. Needless to say, this article was read with outrage by therapists who treat dissociative disorders.

MPD is an intriguing, dramatic disorder which lends itself to sensational portrayals – witness the success of *Sybil,* by Flora Schreiber (Schreiber 1974) and *The Three Faces of Eve* by Corbett Thigpen and Harvey Cleckley (Thigpen and Cleckley 1992) – which unfortunately can also contribute, as one therapist put it, to the 'dynamiting of the entire treatment classification and its therapists' through damaging publicity. As a topic, the media's approach to MPD is as intriguing as the disorder itself.

Within the mental health profession there is considerable disagreement regarding the phenomenon, or the claim, of *recovery* of memories of child abuse. Merskey (1996) reports on the fact that six scientific bodies, including the American Psychiatric Association, the American Psychological Association and the American Medical Association, 'recently struggled with the issue of RM [recovered memories] and produced varied reports. ... The biggest "gap", on which the members clearly disagreed, was the weight to be attached to the possibility of memories being recovered versus the possibility of pseudo-memories being produced' (p.330).

According to Elizabeth Loftus (1996), a leading critic of 'false memory creation',

> In the last decade, hundreds if not thousands of patients have emerged from psychotherapy accusing their fathers and mothers, their uncles and grandfathers, their former neighbors, their former teachers and therapist, and countless others, of sexually abusing them years before... In many cases, accused people have found themselves dragged through the criminal justice system and occasionally, to their shock, sent off to prison. (p.281)

'Frequently,' she continues, 'that process of excavating the "repressed" memories involves invasive therapeutic techniques such as age regression, guided visualization, trance writing, dream work, body work, hypnosis, and sodium amytal or "truth serum"' (p.282). False memories, she states, 'can be induced when a person is encouraged to imagine experiencing specific events without worrying about whether they really happened or not' (1997, p.71).

Davies and Frawley (1994) are among clinicians who strongly disagree with this formulation. 'In discussing the encoding and retrieval of traumatic memories,' they state, 'we enter an era of fierce controversy. Psychoanalytically oriented clinicians, aware of the organizing role of fantasy in a child's life, frequently question the accuracy of childhood memories, traumatic or not, reported by patients. …Trauma research, however, indicates that traumatic memories are indeed retrievable and are essentially accurate' (p.97). Advocating efforts on the part of the therapist to facilitate the disclosure of childhood abuse, they state:

> If secrecy is the mainstay of childhood sexual abuse, disclosure to a validating, believing other is the first step in a process of healing the devastating wounds of early sexual victimization. It is therefore crucial that clinicians know how and when to facilitate disclosure, so that they can become that, often first, validating and believing other. (p.86)

Courtois (1997a; 1997b), responding to issues raised in the recovered/false memory controversy, emphasizes the importance of a neutral stance on the part of the therapist. 'Practitioners,' she states, 'should expect a range of memory presentations and must work to neither suggest nor suppress abuse-related issues that arise in the course of therapy' (1997b, p.497). She lists nineteen 'General Treatment Issues and Recommendations' for the practitioner. 'Professional organizations,' she states, 'are currently devising principles, recommendations, and statements as precursors to the development of standards of practice (for post-trauma treatment in general and for post-abuse and delayed/recovery memory issues) and consequently, clinicians must exercise caution and sensitivity when working with these issues' (1997b, p.498).

The very extent of the guidelines listed by Courtois attests to the extraordinary care with which the therapist is advised to become engaged in treatment where issues pertaining to memory are involved. She includes the advice: 'Do not automatically assume sexual abuse from a set of symptoms' (p.503); 'Do not use hypnosis (or related techniques) for memory retrieval per se' (p.505); and 'Do not encourage or suggest a lawsuit' (p.508). This caveat is reaffirmed by Guttheil (1995), in a statement pertaining to risk management and recovered memories, in which he advises that 'The most useful risk management advice to therapists is to advise patients not to make precipitous and irreversible decisions during treatment, including a hasty decision to enter the legal arena, which requires objective evidentiary reality instead of subjective clinical truth.' He concludes his statement with the comment that 'Our patients are best served by keeping therapy in the office and out of court' (p.537).

Few controversies have stirred antagonism within the mental health profession to the extent of the recovered/false memory issue. In an article on clinicians' practices and beliefs in this area, Palm and Gibson (1998) state:

Besides creating a climate of skepticism about the motives of therapists and the benefits of therapy, the controversy over recovered memories of childhood sexual abuse (CSA) has divided psychologists and may be negatively affecting the treatment of actual CSA victims. (p.257)

This is indeed a deplorable situation. And yet the publicity and the virulence within the profession concerning false memory issues have hopefully resulted in a heightened awareness of tendencies unacknowledged by even the part of the most conscientious practitioners. As Palm and Gibson remind us: 'Therapists might search for evidence that will support their theory of abuse and, thereby, inadvertently influence the type of information the client offers' (p.257). The case of Marta exemplifies this statement.

MARTA: A THERAPIST'S TEMPTATION TO RETRIEVE A MEMORY

In a recent conversation concerning implanted memories a colleague, Dr X, provided a striking example of the seductive nature of *her own hunches* in her work with a nine-year-old girl, Marta. Dr X acknowledged her own temptation to suggest historical abuse in the work with a child whose behavior was puzzling and disruptive and who urged her to help her to find a reason for the aggressive episodes which occasioned her referral for therapy.

Marta was a very appealing child who was adopted at the age of seven by a young childless professional couple. She had spent her first seven years in a crowded, understaffed orphanage in a Third World country, and had no memory of her parents, nor any information concerning her family. Her memories of life in the orphanage, as might be expected, were generally ambivalent; the 'maters,' as she called her caregivers, were strict but for the most part loving women, and she had both positive and negative memories of her 'sisters and brothers.'

At her first appointment Marta greeted Dr X with the plea: 'I want you to find out what makes me so angry at my Mom and Dad.' Her adoptive parents had reported that she was quite agreeable – indeed, a lovable child in most of her interactions with them – but that she 'turned into a witch when it was time for bed.' She suffered from an intense fear of the dark: a fear which was respected by her parents, who installed night lights throughout the sleeping area of the home. She would not discuss her fear with them; rather, she fought her new parents at the very mention of bedtime, and occasionally in her frenzy at the thought of going to bed she resorted to kicking and biting.

Following her announcement to Dr X that she wanted help with her anger, Marta eagerly agreed to draw the bedtime scenes, and produced a surprisingly frank illustration of her own aggression, showing her kicking her father and biting her mother. Marta had considerable artistic talent, and readily agreed to the format of drawing her experiences.

Marta opened the second session by asking: 'Well, do you have any clues yet?' This established the fact that in her mind Dr X's job was that of a detective, in pursuit of a motive for the angry aggression. Her therapist responded by suggesting that 'the two of us need to work on this problem together,' a pronouncement which seemed to please Marta. Dr X then suggested that Marta draw 'bedtime at the orphanage,' a project which Marta embarked upon with some relish.

Using one sheet of paper for each of a sequence of events, Marta produced a cartoon-like depiction of events taking place in the girls' dormitory, portraying two girls, one identified as 'me' and the other as 'my friend.' In the drawings she had been awakened in the night by the need to use the bathroom, which was outside. In accordance with the rules, she awakened her friend to accompany her to the toilet. The two girls were drawn walking in the dark toward the outhouse, with the moon and stars in the upper corner of the page. She then drew herself emerging from the shack, greeted by her sleepy friend.

As Marta began to draw the next scenario, Dr X noticed that the child began to tremble, as she asked, in her native language, for a black crayon. 'This is it,' thought Dr X. 'Marta was assaulted in the night.'

Using the black crayon, Marta then drew the equivalent of a series of expletives, as though an explosion had occurred in the area outside of the outdoor plumbing facility. She then threw the crayon down and stood up, saying 'I'm tired of drawing.' Sensing that she was on the cusp of an important breakthrough, Dr X attempted gently to help Marta explore the memory further, but met with stubborn resistance. The session ended with a game of Checkers.

Marta was never able to elaborate upon this sequence of drawings, and she was not urged to do so. Although it seemed likely that she had suffered a traumatic event which accounted for the aggressive behavior, displaced onto her adoptive parents, *Dr X refrained from suggesting that she had been intruded upon in the dark outside of her dormitory, and that her bedtime aggression was related to a painful episode in 'her country'.*

Marta was eager to understand her own rage, and her fears. Her fear of the dark was indeed a terror. On one occasion, as she sat with Dr X in an early afternoon session, the sun was blanketed for a brief moment by a cloud, causing the room to become somewhat less bright – a change which Dr X did not notice until Marta, in a state of panic, demanded that she turn on the overhead light. 'Can't you tell? It's dark!' she shouted. She could not elaborate upon her fear, and although Dr X sensed that a valuable 'clue' had been lost, she did not press the frightened child to associate to the darkening of the room.

Marta and Dr X were indeed in concert in searching for the source of the explosive behavior. It was as though both felt that the 'tragedy' – the vicious evening tantrums – needed a plot, including a 'bad guy,' to provide a basis for her displaced vengeance. In these circumstances, *the therapist might have suggested an event, with perhaps a perpetrator, which would have accounted for the child's reactions to the dark and to bedtime.* And the child might have complied with the suggestion to ease her own tension, or to please the therapist. And yet Dr X scrupulously avoided suggesting that Marta had been intruded upon, as to do so would have been tantamount to implanting a memory and might have seriously derailed the work. Marta's memories of an incident in the dark, in 'her country,' were intolerable; she could not bear more than a fleeting recollection of the night outside the latrine. Dr X decided to let the matter rest as a therapeutic issue until Marta could feel sufficiently strong to face the presumed memory. At the same time, there was important work to be done with the adoptive parents, who were anxious to learn ways of helping the child to gain a sense of security.

Marta's early experiences took place in a developing country, halfway around the globe; thus, litigation was at no time a consideration in the work with Dr X. There was neither a remembered incident nor an identified perpetrator. Dr X's decisions regarding Marta's treatment, notwithstanding the child's pleas to 'find a clue,' were based upon ethical and personal principles pertaining to the therapist's role in the recall of memories. Sensitive to the bitter controversy within her profession regarding 'false' and 'implanted' memories, and unwilling to intrude further upon a child whose life had already been interrupted and fragmented with little respite, Dr X did not press Marta for associations. At the time of this writing, Marta continues to ask: 'Got any clues?' However, both she and Dr X seem to understand that there will not be a piece of evidence 'that cracks the case.' Perhaps she was intruded upon in the orphanage. Or perhaps she felt that she was kidnaped by her adoptive parents. Whatever the facts, or the fantasies, Dr X's efforts were directed toward working with the new parents while listening carefully for the 'clues' which so intrigued her young patient.

THE SCHREBER CASE

Published between 1951 and 1974, Niederland's studies of the Schreber case, a case described by the former as 'Freud's most important contribution to the psychoanalytic exploration of psychotic illness' (1974, p.xiii), provide remarkable evidence reminding us that we must be alert to 'the kernel of truth' in even the most bizarre delusions and recollections of the disturbed patient. Using evidence gathered several decades after Freud's 1911 publication on the Schreber case, 'Psycho-analytic notes upon an autobiographical account of a case of paranoia', a study of Schreber's *Denkwurdigkeiten eines Nervenkranken* (1903), Niederland discovered that Schreber's delusional fantasies were in fact *distorted memories of realistic experiences in his early life* (1974, p.27).

Schreber's delusions, as reported in his *Denkwurdigkeiten eines Nervenkranken,* concern 'miracles' which he reported as having been constantly performed on his body by God, florid fantasies and hallucinatory experiences. According to Han Israels (1981), although Schreber's memoirs had attracted great interest in psychiatric circles, 'It was not until 1959 that a psychoanalyst at first paid any real attention to Paul Schreber's father' (p.18). Schreber's father, Moritz Schreber, had published works on child rearing, and after researching these works Niederland wrote that 'closer examination of the available sources has convinced me that there is a realistic core in this delusional material... The historical truth about these...miracles can be found in...paternal practices described in Dr Schreber's [the father's] books' (1974, p.76). These practices included the use of orthopedic appliances illustrated in the pages of Niederland's book: machines the sight of which is horrifying to the reader.

Schreber's paranoia and his delusional system become understandable as based upon reality when we learn that:

> On the basis of ample evidence of Dr. Schreber's own writings, it is clear that he also used a 'scientifically' elaborated system of relentless mental and corporeal pressure alternating with occasional indulgence, a methodical sequence of studiously applied terror interrupted by compensatory periods of seductive benevolence and combined with ritual observances that he as a reformer incorporated into his overall missionary scheme of physical edu-cation. (Niederland 1974, p.70)

In addition to the concrete torturous practices described by Dr Schreber, his disciplinary measures, published in a guidebook for parents, will make the reader cringe. These include 'corporal punishment...at the slightest infringement' and a reminder to 'compel the child, when it has been punished, "to stretch out its hand to the executor of the punishment"; this ensures "against the possibility of spite and bitterness"' (Niederland 1974, p.56). This practice, of course, precludes expressions of revenge.

Niederland's research, then, led him to the conviction that 'there is a realistic core in this delusional material' (1974, p.76). He writes of the 'historical truth,' the 'kernel of truth,' and the 'nucleus of truth' in Schreber's delusions. In a 1968 article, 'Schreber and Fleschig: A further contribution to the 'kernel of truth' in Schreber's delusional system,' Niederland urges the clinician to trace the patient's delusions to their sources, be they memories or thoughts related to current situations. Further pursuing the data of the Schreber case, he concluded that 'we are entitled, I think, to recognize in these archaic transference phenomena the regressively distorted, yet still identifiable vestiges of the concrete life experiences of the patient, that is, the "kernel of truth" contained in these delusional formations of his and now uncovered with the aid of a posthumous "mining operation"' (1968, p.743).

These finds alert us to the danger of assuming that memories which appear to be delusional are artifacts created by the processes of the treatment. It cannot be assumed that the therapist has used coercion or even subtle suggestion in the treatment of the seriously disturbed individual who in his treatment retrieves apparently incredible memories. The 'kernel of truth,' difficult as it may be to detect, is a kernel worth diligent pursuit.

CONCLUSIONS

There is no suggestion of 'false memory syndrome' in the Schreber case, as Paul Schreber revealed his delusions in his memoirs, without direction from the professionals who treated him. It has been a phenomenon primarily of the last decade, according to Loftus (1996), that 'various therapeutic interventions excavated the mental contents' of the patient, 'making their presence known' (p.281). Today, a Schreber-like case might eventuate in litigation against a therapist whose therapeutic intervention was seen as 'an excavation of mental contents' of the patient.

Having explored some of the many situations in which the therapist might find himself charged with creating false memories or implanting memories, we must ask ourselves: how do these situations come about? Why would a therapist, consciously or unconsciously (and we prefer to think unconsciously), influence the person who has sought his help in such a way as to *collude in the manufacture of distressing memories*?

Brenneis (1997) states that 'some therapeutically recovered memories may reflect the cherished beliefs of clinicians who recover them' (p.531). In a somewhat less charitable vein, he writes later in the article, 'One cannot dismiss out of hand the awful possibility that the very clinicians who have worked so diligently to free patients from the burden of horrible secret pasts have, at times, succeeded in the opposite, burdening them with a horrible past they did not have. I hope this is not the case, but the problem of false memories cannot be resolved by closing one's eyes to the possibility of powerful, unconscious therapeutic influence (p.544). Few therapists would like to think of themselves as motivated by a desire for power or influence. And yet, we sometimes do convey that image. Why else does the distressed husband say: 'I resent her therapist. He turned her against me!' Or who has not heard the parent protest: 'He'll do anything his therapist advises him to do!'?

Sexual misconduct

Like any other breach of ethics in the psychotherapist's practice, sexual misconduct must be taken in context. The ambiguity of the term is amusingly illustrated in a statement by Gutheil and Gabbard (1993), who comment that

'From the viewpoint of current risk-management principles, a handshake is about the limit of social physical contact at this time. Of course, a patient who attempts a hug in the last session after 7 years of intense, intensive, and successful therapy should probably not be hurled across the room' (p.195).

In this statement it is the word 'risk' which must be taken very seriously, and accordingly the literature is replete with articles concerning *prevention* of behavior, in the sexual sphere, which constitutes boundary violation. Most of the articles urge that training programs for mental health professionals include explicit guidelines for ethical behavior in this area, with information concerning the possible consequences of violations of standards. In an article stressing prevention, or 'avoiding the slippery slope' leading to psychotherapist sexual misconduct, Strasburger, Jorgenson and Sutherland (1992) begin by stating that 'the extent of the practice' of psychotherapist-patient sexual contact 'is shocking' (p.544). Much of their advice relates to the education of mental health professionals, with the elucidation of the characteristics of the 'slippery slope' – the fact that 'in a common scenario, therapy proceeds through a gradual blurring of boundaries…that provide structure to the therapy.' 'When the boundaries erode, 'the principle of abstinence disappears. Reasons for abstaining from sexual relations become lost as the therapy founders on the shoals of impulse' (p.547).

The authors stress how the *power imbalance* between therapist and patient can lead to boundary violations. The therapist has 'advantages of education, experience, status and authority' (Strasburger *et al.*, p.545), placing him in a position in which exploitation is all too easy. Epstein and Simon (1990; and Kay 1992) have formulated an 'Exploitation Index,' or 'an early warning indicator of boundary violations in psychotherapy': a self-assessment questionnaire by which a therapist may evaluate himself with reference to such traits as power seeking, eroticism, exhibitionism and greediness.

The therapist who becomes sexually involved with his or her clients is of course not necessarily an exploitative individual with a lust for power. It would thus seem useful to explore the subtle, less conscious motivations which may lead to the 'gradual erosion of boundaries'. A study by Gabbard on sexual boundary violations (1996) explores a number of unconscious reasons for the gradual crossing of boundaries: for example, 'misguided efforts to love the patient back to health' (p.314). Gabbard writes,

> Consider, for example, the decision to hug a patient. Such decisions are often based on a conscious intention of demonstrating caring for the patient. A male therapist hugging a female patient may conceptualize his action as providing 'maternal nurturance' to a patient who is viewed as suffering from deficits secondary to childhood neglect. Such a conceptualization can be a convenient way of rationalizing the gratification of the therapist's own needs to be loved (and held) by the patient. (p.313)

In the same vein, recognizing the therapist's narcissistic needs, Gabbard states: 'That wish for exclusivity (i.e. to be the patient's "one and only" love object) may be a powerful unconscious factor in accepting the patient's love at face value. For some therapists, it is too painful to acknowledge that similar feelings would come up with any other therapist' (p.318).

Gabbard concludes with advice which runs through the literature on the subject of sexual boundary violations: *the importance of consultation*, and the need for openness in this area. 'The thoughts, feelings, and behaviors that a therapist would most like to keep secret from a supervisor or consultant,' he states, 'are the most important issues to discuss with that supervisor or consultant' (p.321).

The Bean-Bayog case: Questions of sexual misconduct and recovered memories

Perhaps the most damaging case on record – damaging both to the therapist and to the mental health profession, because of the media spectacle it generated – was the Bean-Bayog case, in which a 49-year-old female psychiatrist was sued by the family of a patient, a young male medical student who committed suicide after she had terminated his treatment, and while he was in treatment with another therapist. Bean-Bayog was accused of sexually seducing her patient – sexually enslaving him, in fact – and of creating an environment in the treatment whereby memories of childhood incest were 'created.'

Dr Bean-Bayog, feeling that irreparable damage had been done by the charges and the publicity, and threatened by the prospect of ruinous legal fees, resigned her license to practice medicine, and the case never went to court. It was not until the sensational reporting began to die down that members of the mental health profession began to express their outrage at the destructive manner in which the case had been handled and reported. Among others who wrote critically of the handling of the case were Maltsberger (1993), who was called into the case as an expert witness, Waldinger (1993), a potential expert witness, and Chafetz and Chafetz (1994), an investigative reporter and his psychiatrist father, who gained exclusive interviews with Dr Bean-Bayog.

Maltsberger, who stated that he wished to 'put some fairer perspectives on what I believe was an act of arson by the press' (1993, p.290), believed that after the treatment had been terminated, the patient 'lied about the treatment to avenge himself on Dr Bean-Bayog for declining to see him any longer.' Maltsberger reminds the reader that the patient had stolen some of his personal records from his psychiatrist's office, and states, 'I would have stopped the treatment at this juncture, but, as Hippocrates said, judgment is difficult' (p.288).

Waldinger, who said of the case that it was 'every psychiatrist's nightmare come true,' comments primarily upon the damage done to psychiatry as a profession when there are court hearings, which are adversarial processes by nature.

'Public discussion of intimate details of a psychotherapy,' he states, 'shakes the foundation of privacy on which treatment rests and, with it, people's trust in the confidentiality of such treatment' (1993, p.62).

In discussions of the Bean-Bayog case, the question of recovered memories has received less attention than has sexual misconduct, although there were suggestions, on the part of the plaintiffs, that the topic of incestuous relations in the patient's childhood was spearheaded by the therapist rather than by the patient. In this area, Bean-Bayog is defended only ambiguously. In Chafetz and Chafetz's book, *Obsession: The Bizarre Relationship Between a Prominent Harvard Psychiatrist and her Suicidal Patient* (1994), the author/reporter states that a source told him 'that the hypothesis of childhood sexual abuse bore more validity if first advanced by the patient, less so if advanced by the therapist' (p.316). A rather mild defense.

However supportive the above-quoted authors prove to be in their writing about the case, they invariably agree that the psychiatrist became over-involved in her treatment of the young male medical student. Also, it was generally felt that she did not take adequate precautions on her own behalf. Many therapists would not have undertaken the treatment of an individual whose history clearly indicated suicidal tendencies, as did Bean-Bayog's patient, who had made many suicidal gestures or attempts, beginning in childhood. In referring to the work with suicidal patients, Kernberg (1993) states that an essential aspect of the therapy with these individuals is that:

> The therapist should feel physically and psychologically safe, legally protected, and although he/she obviously wishes to keep the patient alive, it is important that the therapist is recommending a treatment in which there is always a risk that the patient might end up committing suicide. The therapist is willing to undertake the treatment under these conditions with the implicit understanding that the therapist will not be more responsible than the patient himself for keeping the patient alive. (p.252)

It is hard to imagine a more damaging charge than that leveled against Dr Bean-Bayog. In essence, she was accused of seducing her patient and driving him to suicide. It is heartening to read the articles and books written in defense of the therapist. Yet it is both sobering and troubling to be reminded of the risks taken by the individual who chooses to dedicate his energies to becoming a member of the *helping profession*.

Managed care: The therapist as plaintiff

At a recent meeting of psychologists recognizing outgoing and incoming board members, as the outgoing president presented the newly elected child officer with a handsome gavel, one of the members in the audience quipped: 'Who are you going to hit with it?', whereupon the new president replied almost reflexively: 'Managed care.' Revenge, indeed!

A more formal statement of the mental health professional's antagonism toward managed care is that of Martin E.P. Seligman, President, and Ronald F. Levant, Recording Secretary of the American Psychological Association:

> In the past decade, health care corporations have been aggressively driving down costs. Psychological expenditures are increasingly restricted by routing patients to less well trained caregivers and by only authorizing brief therapy. Being an experienced, highly trained doctoral-level psychologist who is skilled in long term therapy has become a disadvantage, rather than an asset, in today's market.
>
> Independent practice has been hurt as services becomes subject to pre-authorization and intensive review and as *medically necessary* comes to mean the bare restoration of functioning. Public sector practitioners are also hurt as government embraces managed care and embarks on privatization, drastically reducing jobs.
>
> Is there empirical justification for cutting length of therapy and lowering the qualifications of mental health providers? We think not. And we conclude managed care organizations (MCOs) have seized on inappropriate and inadequate data to rationalize their downsizing of mental health care. Critical to our thinking is the distinction between *efficiency* and *effectiveness* in psychotherapy outcome research. (1998, p.211)

However his outrage is expressed, the therapist has in the past decade found himself in a position quite similar to that of many of his clients: faced with the intrusion of powerful forces threatening privacy and autonomy. A key difference between the position of the client and that of the endangered therapist, however, lies in the fact that many of our clients, and here I refer primarily to the Exploited-Repressive individual, have only slowly recognized the exploitation or misuse of power on the part of the parental figure, whereas the mental health professional has experienced a sudden onslaught by the powerful forces of managed care. And unlike his patient, the therapist is finding strong and dedicated support in his battle.

The coalitions and the associations

As a psychologist/psychotherapist practicing in the Greater Washington Metropolitan Area, I receive innumerable publications from professional coalitions and associations, in which there are an increasing number of articles dealing with the threats of managed care. To demonstrate the flavor of practitioners' feelings on this issue, and their thirst for vindication, I have quoted passages from some recent statements by representatives of several organizations.

1. From the Practice Directorate of the American Psychological Association: an excerpt from a letter written by Russ Newman, Ph.D., J.D., the APA Executive Director for Professional Practice, 3 November 1997, citing recent court decisions regarding managed care, and favorable to the mental health profession:

> Without question, the growing emphasis on cost containment, managed care and corporate profits continues to take its toll on psychologists and their patients... However, we have witnessed and actively participated in a number of significant recent developments that have the potential to restore psychologists' capacity for decision making and to stimulate the necessary emphasis on quality health care.

2. An excerpt from a letter to members of the Virginia Academy of Clinical Psychologists, written by Michael S. Weissman, Ph.D., President, and Elizabeth A. Hauck, Ph.D., President-Elect of VACP, 5 May 1998:

> As part of the service provided to our membership, the Virginia Academy of Psychologists (VACP) monitors and collects information on managed care companies. In part, our goal is to identify action taken by managed care companies which we believe may threaten the interests of our membership, the profession of psychology, the psychologist-patient relationship or the public interest.

The authors then inform the membership that VACP has engaged the services of a law firm to help gather and review information from psychologists regarding one of the major Health Maintenance Organizations, in an effort to determine whether the HMO's conduct may have violated any legal obligations.

3. Excerpts from a letter to members of the D.C. Psychological Association written by Larney R. Gump, Ed.D., Interim Chair Public Education Task Force, 6 March 1997, urging members to join a public education campaign on managed care's invasions in the field of psychology: 'The tide of managed care can be altered!' The author of the letter suggests Public Outreach – speaking to civic and business organizations – and stresses the need to get the message across 'through print [media], radio and TV.' 'Managed care is affecting all of us,' he concludes, and asks, 'How can we passively allow it to roll over us, changing our clinical practice and integrity as providers of care?'

4. An excerpt from a brochure distributed by The National Coalition of Mental Health Professionals and Consumers, Inc., a 'national grass-roots action organization of mental health professionals and consumer advocates...dedicated to fighting the negative impact of managed care on both clients and professionals, while advocating for fair and reasonable health care reform.' The brochure states:

> The National Coalition is doing well in the battle with Goliath. It has begun waking America up to the problems in managed mental health care through media exposes, mobilizing professional organizations, and educating

legislators. The National Coalition is a major force exposing the abuses in managed mental health care, and it is the loudest and clearest voice.

5. An excerpt from a speech by Karen Shore, National Coalition president, the keynote speaker at a legislative conference of the Greater Washington Coalition of Mental Health Professionals and Consumers, Inc.: 'Why believe that managed care is here to stay? Rome fell. The Holy Roman Empire fell. Nazi Germany fell. Why not believe that all totalitarian regimes eventually fail?'

Some individual warriors

Bryant Welch, J.D., Ph.D., a psychologist and attorney, the founder and first Executive Director of the American Psychological Association Practice Directorate, and one of the most outspoken critics of the managed care industry, recently established one of the first nationally based law practices devoted exclusively to managed care abuses. Writing in *Psychologist-Psychoanalyst*, the official publication of Division 39 of the American Psychological Association, Welch states in an article entitled 'Suing managed-care companies: the work begins' (1996, pp.6–8) that 'Over the past several months I have filed four lawsuits against major managed-care companies and have been able to help numerous other patients obtain badly needed treatment through more informal negotiation.' 'Filing serious lawsuits,' he states, 'provides impetus for the companies to negotiate in good faith on subsequent matters with other patients. Similarly, managed care companies are terrified of "winding up on *60 Minutes*," as one spokesperson put it.'

Stanley Moldawsky (1997), President of Division 42 (Independent Practice) of the American Psychological Association, in an article entitled 'Managed care and psychotherapy are incompatible,' states that 'The implication of [managed care's] rationing of care is that the patient is not getting what he needs, but is getting what they decide he needs. [Their decision is not based on his need, but rather on saving money.]' APA groups, however, states Moldawsky, are fighting back, through a task force. 'Our efforts,' he states, 'are working. The media is publishing articles about folks who have been mistreated by the system.'

Sandra Boodman, a *Washington Post* staff writer, in an article entitled 'Are patients getting what they need' (1997), presents chilling examples of two adolescent boys who were denied hospitalization by the managed care organizations in which they were enrolled, although they had shown unmistakable suicidal tendencies. One of the youngsters completed suicide; the other was repeatedly hospitalized in institutions which were financed by Medicaid. Boodman, not herself a mental health professional, interviewed a number of psychiatrists and psychologists who were quite forthcoming in their indictments of managed care and in expressing their own frustrations.

As a member of a coalition group protested, 'We're not used to this kind of war.' True: unless he entered the mental health field very recently, the therapist has had little reason to anticipate that there would be a powerful assault upon his profession. *By and large, it seems safe to state that he chose to be a psychologist, a psychiatrist, a social worker or a counselor because he was interested in the intricacies of the human mind, and in helping troubled persons. He did not choose big business or politics or law as his career: he is not likely to be adversarial by temperament.* We often hear it stated that individuals enter the mental health field in order to resolve personal conflicts or with the hope of healing wounds inflicted in the past. A study by Paris and Frank (1983) indicates that psychotherapists, like members of the medical profession, often base their career choice upon a wish to make reparation for disturbances in their families of origin; they have a need to be a buffer and a helper for others. (p.356)

Waldinger (1993), referring to malpractice risks, makes a statement which is also appropriate to the problem of managed care when he writes: 'Psychotherapists are not, by nature, activists, but we need to be active on several fronts' (p.63). Some of our most ardent champions in the managed care battle are gentle, reflective persons who treasure privacy. And perhaps at some expense to their own comfort, these therapists, as well as their more feisty colleagues, are stepping into the fray, individually or in groups, crying '*Vengeance is mine!*' – or perhaps more accurately, '*Vengeance is ours!*'

It is indeed impressive to behold the fervor with which psychotherapist colleagues rise to the occasion in refuting the practices of managed care organizations: colleagues whom we associate with study groups for underprivileged children, or strategies for ameliorating depression in the nursing home. And it is perhaps surprising, but also reassuring, to be reminded that the therapist's aggression, normally fairly adequately sublimated, is ready to be kindled when his profession, his ethical standards and his patients' well-being are threatened.

Conclusions

As Galdston (1987) rather pithily states it, 'There are no statutes of limitation on the law of the talion' (p.371). Revenge can be endless, consuming time, energy and creativity. Of forgiveness, on the other hand, Galdston says: 'With forgiveness, the blocking introject loses its significance. The goal of revenge passes. Comfort in a stronger ego allows the patient the prospect of a future freed of hatred from the past' (p.377).

In these chapters we have considered a variety of manifestations of revenge encountered by the therapist in his work with the Exploited-Repressive individual and with the Vindictive Character; with adults, adolescents and children, with the criminal population and in the legal arena. In addition, we have noted some 'slippery slopes' in each aspect of the therapist's work: the possibility of 'professional coasting' or 're-exploitation' with the Exploited-Repressive patient, for example; the difficulties, among others, of dealing with devaluation and the negative therapeutic reaction in the work with the Vindictive Character; and the special skills and tolerances necessary in working with the small child who communicates primarily through metaphor, or with the incarcerated offender who attempts to 'con' his therapist into helping him achieve his overriding goal: release from confinement.

Forgiveness, if it is an issue in psychotherapy, has myriad meanings, according to the experience of both the patient and the therapist. Acts of forgiveness and of apology may be perfunctory, eliciting resentment, or they may involve a sincere, perhaps painful and laborious process of resolution, similar to the process of mourning. When and if the question of forgiveness is addressed as part of the therapeutic process, it is essential that the therapist be aware of both his own and his patient's biases regarding the meaning of forgiveness.

The revenge component is usually all too clear in the work with the Vindictive Character, who comes wearing his vengefulness on his sleeve. Likewise, one does not have to ferret out the revenge ingredient in much forensic work, and in defending malpractice suits. With the Exploited-Repressive patient, on the other hand, it often happens that the therapist recognizes the exploitations experienced by the patient, becomes indignant and finds himself entertaining revenge fantasies long before the patient himself becomes aware of the fact that he has been used.

In the work with the child, and to some extent with the adolescent, the therapist must often call upon his skills as detective/translator in determining toward whom and for what reason the young patient is directing his resentment. Refusal to eat, for example, may have little to do with the appeal of the food offered.

In forensic work, the therapist meets revenge in its least subtle form. In the practice of forensic psychotherapy vindictiveness is likely a central issue; and in adversarial situations – in the courts, as an expert witness, as a defendant in a malpractice suit, or as a plaintiff in a suit against managed care – the word 'adversary' says it all. (As Webster would have it: 'One who opposes another, esp. with animosity.')

There may be an element of revenge, often fairly obscure, in the patient's symptoms, and it is useful for the therapist to keep this in mind as he listens to his patient. When considering forgiveness, on the other hand, there is not the question of a mystery for the therapist and the patient to explore. Forgiveness is a process. Forgiveness is not inevitable; in some situations it is not thought to be appropriate. To forgive may be painful. But forgiveness, sincere and thoughtfully considered, can ultimately be liberating.

The rewards of exploring the components of revenge and forgiveness in psychotherapy are many. To the extent that he can become freed of the need to seek vengeance, the patient has paradoxically triumphed in a battle which has consumed his energies. And to the extent that he may have forgiven his perpetrator, he has helped to create the possibility of a new dimension in a troubled relationship.

References

Abstracts, (1972) *The Psychoanalytic Study of the Child*, Vols. 1–25. C.L. Rothgeb (ed) National Clearing House for Mental Health Information.

Acocella, J. (1998) 'The politics of hysteria.' *New Yorker*, 6 April, 64–97.

Alter, J. (1997) 'The long shadow of slavery.' *Newsweek*, 8 December, 58–63.

Anastaspoulos, D. and Tsiantis, J. (1996) 'Countertransference issues in psychoanalytic psychotherapy with children and adolescents: A brief review.' In J. Tsiantis, A., Sandler, D. Anastasopoulos and B. Martindale (eds) *Countertransference in Psychoanalytic Psychotherapy with Children and Adolescents* (pp.1–35). Madison: CT International Universities Press, Inc.

Andrews, M. (1994) *Dickens and the Grown-Up Child*. Iowa City, Iowa: University of Iowa Press.

Anthony, E.J. (1969) 'The reactions of adults to adolescents and their behavior.' In G. Capland and S. Lebovici (eds) *Adolescent Psychosocial Perspectives*. New York: Basic Books.

Anthony, E.J. (1972) 'An experimental approach to the psychopathology of childhood encopresis.' In Harrison and McDermott (eds) *Childhood Psychopathology*, (pp. 610–627). New York: International Universities Press.

Anthony, E.J. (1974) 'The syndrome of the psychologically invulnerable child.' In E.J. Anthony and C. Koujpernik (eds) *The Child in his Family: Children at Psychiatric Risk*. International Yearbook, (Vol. 3) New York: Wiley.

Anthony, E.J. (1986) 'The contributions of child psychoanalysts to psychoanalysis.' *The Psychoanalytic Study of the Child 41*, 61–87. New York: International Universities Press.

Appelbaum, P.S. (1997) 'Ethics in evolution: the incompatibility of clinical and forensic functions.' *American Journal of Psychiatry and the Law 154*, 4, 445–446.

Arvin, N. (1950) *Herman Melville*. USA: William Sloane Associates.

Atwood, M. (1993) *The Robber Bride*. New York: Doubleday.

Azar, B. (1977) 'Forgiveness helps keep relationships steadfast.' *APA Monitor*, November, p.14.

Baker, H. and Wills, U. (1978) 'School phobia: Classification and treatment.' *British Journal of Psychiatry 132*, 492–499.

Baker, P. (1990) 'Teen's suicide: "The ultimate act of revenge against the world".' *Washington Post*, 4 May.

Barreca, R. (1995) *Sweet Revenge: The Wicked Delights of Getting Even*. New York: Harmony Books.

Baudry, F. (1991) 'The relevance of the analyst's character and attitudes to his work.' *Journal of the American Psychoanalytic Association 39*, 917–938.

Bazelon, D.L. (1978) 'The role of the psychiatrist in the criminal justice system.' *Bulletin of the American Academy of Psychiatry and the Law 6*, 2, 139–146.

Bemporad, J.R. and Gabel, S. (1992) 'Depressed and suicidal children and adolescents.' In J.R. Brandell (ed) *Countertransference in Psychotherapy with Children and Adolescents*. New Jersey: Jason Aronson.

Bloom, H. (1986) *Modern Critical Views. Herman Melville*. New York: Chelsea House Publishers.

Blum, H.P. (1997) 'Clinical and developmental dimensions of hate.' *Journal of the American Psychoanalytic Association 45*, 2, 358–375.

Boodman, S.G. (1997) 'Are patients getting what they need?' *Washington Post*, Health Section, 6 May, 12–15.

Bowlby, J. (1960) 'Grief and mourning in infancy and early childhood.' In *The Psychoanalytic Study of the Child 15*, 9–52. New York: International Universities Press.

Bowlby, J. (1980) *Loss, Sadness and Depression*. New York: Basic Books, Inc.

Brandell, J.R. (ed) (1992) *Countertransference in Psychotherapy with Children and Adolescents.* New Jersey: Jason Aronson.

Brenneis, C.B. (1996) 'Retrieval of memories of trauma.' *Journal of the American Psychoanalytic Association 44,* 4, 1169–1187.

Brenneis, C.B. (1997) 'Final report of APA working group on investigation of memories of childhood abuse: A critical commentary.' *Psychoanalytic Psychology 14,* 4, 531–547.

Bruch, H. (1973) 'Anorexia nervosa.' In *Adolescent Psychiatry,* Volume V, S.C. Feinstein and P. Giovacchini (eds) New York: Jason Aronson.

Burke, N. and Cohler, B.J. (1992) 'Psychodynamic psychotherapy of eating disorders.' In J.R. Brandell (ed) *Countertransference in Psychotherapy with Children and Adolescents.* New Jersey: Jason Aronson.

Caplan, L. (1984) *The Insanity Defense and the Trial of John W. Hinckley, Jr.* Boston: David R. Godine, Publisher.

Carney, F.J. (1971) 'Evaluation of psychotherapy in a maximum security prison.' *Seminars in Psychiatry 3,* 3, 357–362.

Cather, W. (1994) *My Antonia.* New York: Penguin.

Chafetz, G.S. and Chafetz, M.E. (1994) *Obsession: The Bizarre Relationship Between a Prominent Harvard Psychiatrist and her Suicidal Patient.* New York: Crown Publishers, Inc.

Clarke, J.W. (1990) *On Being Mad or Merely Angry.* New Jersey: Princeton University Press.

Coen, S.J. (1997) 'How to help patients (and analysts) bear the unbearable: Paradoxes in psychoanalytic technique.' In press.

Collodi, C. (Carlo Lorenzini) (1946) *The Adventures of Pinoccio.* New York: Grosset and Dunlap.

Cook, S.C. (1996) 'Forensic child and adolescent psychiatry.' *New Directions for Mental Health Services 69,* 15–24.

Cordess, C. (1997) 'Our responsibilities as forensic psychotherapists.' In H. Van Marle (ed) *Challenges in Forensic Psychotherapy.* London: Jessica Kingsley Publishers, Ltd.

Cose, E. (1997) 'Memories in blood.' *Newsweek,* 8 December.

Courtois, C.A. (1997a) 'Healing the incest wound: A treatment update with attention to recovered-memory issues.' *American Journal of Psychotherapy 51,* 4, 464–496.

Courtois, C.A. (1997b) 'Guidelines for the treatment of adults abused or possibly abused as children (with attention to issues of delayed/recovery memory).' *American Journal of Psychotherapy 51,* 4, 497–510.

Courtois, C.A. and Weisstub, D.N. (1996) 'Sexuality in the mental health system.' *International Journal of Law and Psychiatry 19,* 2, 183–190.

Crawford, C. (1978) *Mommie Dearest.* New York: William Morrow.

Crosby, G. (1983) *Going My Own Way.* Garden City, NY: Doubleday.

Cumming, R.G. and Soloway, H.J. (1973) 'The incarcerated psychiatrists.' *Hospital and Community Psychiatry 24,* 9, 631–632.

Daniels, M. (1967) 'Further observations on the development of the vindictive character.' *American Journal of Psychotherapy 21,* 822–831.

Daniels, M. (1969) 'Pathological vindictiveness and the vindictive character.' *Psychoanalytic Review 56,* 169–196.

Davies, J.M. and Frawley, M.G. (1994) *Treating the Adult Survivor of Childhood Sexual Abuse: A Psycho-analytic Perspective.* New York: Basic Books.

Davis, M. and Wallbridge, D. (1981) *Boundary and Space. An Introduction to the Work of D.W. Winnicott.* New York: Brunner/Mazel.

Davis, P. (1992) *The Way I See It.* New York: Putnam.

De Folch, T.E. (1991) 'Obstacles to analytic cure.' In J. Sandler (ed) *On Freud's Analysis Terminable and Interminable.* New Haven and London: Yale University Press.

Deutsch, H. (1942) 'Some forms of emotional disturbance and their relationship to schizophrenia.' *Psychoanalytic Quarterly 11,* 301–321.

Dietz, P.E. (1996) 'The quest for excellence in forensic psychiatry.' *Bulletin of the American Academy of Psychiatry and the Law 24*, 2, 153–163.

DSM IV Diagnostic Criteria (1994) Washington D.C.: American Psychiatric Association.

Durham, M.S. (1978) *An Inquiry into Personality Variables Distinguishing Between Psychotherapists Who Choose to Treat Schizophrenics and Psychotherapists Who Choose to Treat Non-Schizophrenics.* Doctoral Dissertation, University of Maryland Human Development Department.

Durham, M.S. (1990) 'The therapist and the concept of revenge: The law of talion.' *The Journal of Pastoral Care 44*, 131–137.

Ednie, K.J. (1996) 'Challenges for women in forensic psychiatry.' *New Directions for Mental Health Services 69*, 49–57.

Elkind, S.N. (1996) 'The impact of negative experiences as a patient on my work as a therapist.' In B. Gerson (ed) *The Therapist as a Person.* Hillsdale, N.J.: The Analytic Press.

Epstein, R.S. and Simon, R.I. (1990) 'The Exploitation Index: an early warning indicator of boundary violations in psychotherapy.' *Bulletin of the Menninger Clinic 54*, 4, 450–465.

Epstein, R.S., Simon, R.I. and Kay, G.G. (1992) 'Assessing boundary violations in psychotherapy: Survey results with the Exploitation Index.' *Bulletin of the Menninger Clinic 56*, 92, 150–166.

Estrada-Hollenbeck M. and Heatherton, T.F. (1997) 'Avoiding and alleviating guilt through prosocial behavior.' In J. Bybee (ed) *Guilt and Children.* Orlando, Fla: Academic Press.

Finell, J.S. (1985) 'Narcissistic problems in analysts.' *International Journal of Psychoanalysis 66*, 433–445.

Fletcher, M.A. (1997) 'For Americans, nothing is simple about making apology for slavery.' *Washington Post*, 5 August, p.A7.

Forward, S. (1989) *Toxic Parents: Overcoming Their Hurtful Legacy and Reclaiming Your Life.* New York: Bantam Books.

Fraiberg, S. (1982) 'Pathological defenses in infancy.' *Psychoanalytic Quarterly 51*, 612–635.

Freud, A. (1949) 'Aggression in relation to emotional development, normal and pathological.' *The Psychoanalytic Study of the Child 3–4*, 37–42. New York: International Universities Press.

Freud, A. (1960) Discussion of Dr. Bowlby's paper, In *The Psychoanalytic Study of the Child 15*, 53–60. New York: International Universities Press.

Freud, S. (1911) 'Psychoanalytic notes on an autobiographical account of a case of paranoia (dementia paranoides).' In *The Standard Edition of the Complete Psychological Works of Sigmund Freud, Vol. 12.* London: The Hogarth Press.

Freud, S. (1932) *The Interpretation of Dreams* (Completely revised third edition). London: George Allen and Unwin, Ltd.

Freud, S. (1937) 'Analysis terminable and interminable.' In *The Standard Edition of the Complete Psychological Works of Sigmund Freud, Vol. 23.* London: The Hogarth Press.

Freud, S. (1955a) 'Analysis of a phobia in a five-year-old boy.' In *The Standard Edition of the Complete Psychological Works of Sigmund Freud, Vol. 10.* London: The Hogarth Press.

Freud, S. (1955b) 'A case of homosexuality in a woman.' In *The Standard Edition of the Complete Psychological Works of Sigmund Freud, Vol. 18.* London: The Hogarth Press.

Freud, S. (1959) 'Mourning and melancholia.' In *The Standard Edition of the Complete Psychological Works of Sigmund Freud, Vol. 14.* London: The Hogarth Press.

Fromm-Reichmann, F. (1949) 'Personal and professional requirements of a psychotherapist.' *Psychiatry 12*, 361–378.

Furman, E. (1984) 'Some difficulties in assessing depression and suicide in childhood.' In H.S. Sudak, A.B. Ford and N.B. Rushforth (eds) *Suicide in the Young.* (pp.245–258). Boston: John Wright.

Gabbard, G.O. (1989) 'Patients who hate.' *Psychiatry 52*, 96–106.

Gabbard, G.O. (1996) 'Lessons to be learned from the study of sexual boundary violations.' *American Journal of Psychotherapy 50*, 3, 311–321.

Gabbard, G.O. and Lester, E.P. (1995) *Boundaries and Boundary Violations in Psychoanalysis.* N.Y.: Basic Books.

Galdston, R. (1987) 'The longest pleasure: A psychoanalytic study of hatred.' *International Journal of Psychoanalysis 68*, 371–378.

Gallagher, W. (1996) *I.D. How Heredity and Experience Make You Who You Are.* New York: Random House.

Garmezy, N. (1983) 'Stressors of childhood.' In N. Garmezy and M. Rutter (eds) *Stress, Coping, and Development in Children.* (pp.43–84) New York: McGraw-Hill.

Gartner, J. (1992) 'The capacity to forgive: an object relations perspective.' In M. Finn and J. Gartner (eds) *Object Relations Theory and Religion: Clinical Applications.* Westport, CT: Praeger Publishers/ Greenwood Publishing Group, Inc.

Gay, P. (1988) *Freud: A Life for Our Time.* New York: W.W. Norton and Company.

Glickauf-Hughes, C. and Mehlman, E. (1995) 'Narcissistic issues in therapists: Diagnostic and treatment considerations.' *Psychotherapy 32*, 2, 213–221.

Godfrind, J. (1996) 'The influence of the presence of parents on the countertransference of the child psychotherapist.' In J. Tsiantis, A. Sandler, D. Anastasopoulos and B. Martindale (eds) (pp.95–110) *Countertransference in Psychoanalytic Psychotherapy with Children and Adolescents.* Madison, CT: International Universities Press, Inc.

Gopnik, A. (1998) 'Man goes to see a doctor.' *New Yorker,* 24 and 31 August, 114–121.

Gutheil, T.G. (1995) 'Taking issue: Risk management and recovered memories.' *Psychiatric Services 46*, 6, 537.

Gutheil, T.G. and Gabbard, G.O. (1993) 'The concept of boundaries in clinical practice: Theoretical and risk-management dimensions.' *American Journal of Psychiatry 150*, 2, 188–196.

Hartman, H., Kris, E. and Loewenstein, R. (1947) 'Notes on the theory of aggression.' *The Psychoanalytic Study of the Child 3–4.* New York: International Universities Press, Inc. (pp.9–36.)

Heimann, P. (1950) 'On counter-transference.' *International Journal of Psychoanalysis 31*, 81–84.

Herman, J. (1992) *Trauma and Recovery.* USA: Basic Books, Inc.

Herman, S.P. (1990) 'Forensic child psychiatry.' *Journal of the American Academy of Child and Adolescent Psychiatry 29*, 6, 955–957.

Hersov, L.A. (1960a) 'Persistent non-attendance at school.' *Journal of Child Psychology and Psychiatry 1*, 130–136.

Hersov, L.A. (1960b) 'Refusal to go to school.' *Journal of Child Psychology and Psychiatry 1*, pp.137–145.

Hinckley, J. and Hinckley, J., with Sherrill, E. (1985) *Breaking Points.* Grand Rapids, Michigan: Chosen Books.

Horney, K. (1936) 'The problem of the negative therapeutic reaction.' *Psychoanalytic Quarterly 5*, 29–44.

Horney, K. (1948) 'The value of vindictiveness.' *American Journal of Psychoanalysis 8*, 3–12.

Horney, K. (1950) *Neurosis and Human Growth.* New York: W.W. Norton and Co., Inc.

Horowitz, M.J. (1989) 'A model of mourning: Changes in schemas of self and other.' In D.R. Dietrich and P.C. Madison (eds) *The Problem of Loss and Mourning: Psychoanalytic Perspectives.* Madison, CT: International Universities Press.

Hunter, R. (1978) 'Forgiveness, retaliation and paranoid reactions.' *Journal of the Canadian Psychiatric Association 23*, 267–273.

Huth, A. (1994) 'Mistral.' *New Yorker,* 18 May.

Hyde, M.H. (1997) *The Sexual Abuse of Children and Adolescents.* Brookfield, CT: The Milbrook Press.

Hyman, B.D. (1985) *My Mother's Keeper.* New York: Morrow.

Isreals, H. (1981) *Schreber: Father and Son.* Amsterdam: University of Amsterdam.

Jacoby, S. (1983) *Wild Justice: The Evolution of Revenge.* New York: Harper and Row.

Joseph, B. (1989) 'Addiction to near-death.' In M. Feldman and E. Bott-Spillius (eds) *Psychic Equilibrium and Psychic Change.* New York: Tavistock-Routledge. pp.127–138.

Joyce, J. (1992) *A Portrait of the Artist as a Young Man.* New York: Bantam Books.

Kapp, F.T. (1968) 'Ezra Pound's creativity and treason: Clues from his life and work.' *Comprehensive Psychiatry 9*, 4, 414–427.

Karush, A. (1968) 'Working through.' *Psychoanalytic Quarterly* 36, 497–531.

Kernberg, O.F. (1994) 'Aggression, trauma, and hatred in the treatment of borderline patients.' *Psychiatric Clinics of North America* 17, 4, 701–714.

Kernberg, O.F. (1993) 'Suicidal behavior in borderline patients: Diagnosis and psychotherapeutic considerations.' *American Journal of Psychotherapy* 47, 2, 245–254.

Kirman, W.J. (1989) 'Revenge and accommodation in the family.' *Modern Psychoanalysis* 4, 89–95.

Klein, M. (1975a) *Envy and Gratitude.* New York: The Free Press.

Klein, M. (1975b) *Love, Guilt and Reparation and Other Works, 1921–1945.* USA: Delacorte Press/Seymour Lawrence.

Knapp, H.D. (1989) 'Projective identification: Whose projection – whose identity?' *Psychoanalytic Psychology* 6, 47–58.

Kohut, H. (1972) 'Thoughts on narcissism and narcissistic rage.' *The Psychoanalytic Study of the Child 27,* 360–400.

LaMothe, R., Arnold, J. and Crane, J. (1998) 'The penumbra of religious discourse.' *Psychoanalytic Psychology 15,* 63–73.

Lane, R.C. (1985) 'The difficult patient: Resistance and the negative therapeutic reaction: A review.' *Current Issues in Psychoanalytic Practice 1,* 83–106.

Lane, R.C. (1986) 'The recalcitrant supervisee: the negative supervisory reaction.' In H.S. Strean (ed) *Psychoanalysis: The Possible Profession. Current Issues in Psychoanalytic Practice,* Vol. 2. Binghampton, NY: The Haworth Press, Inc.

Lane, R.C. (1995) 'The revenge motive: A developmental perspective on the life cycle and the treatment process.' *Psychoanalytic Review 82,* 1, 41–64.

Lane, R.C., Hull, J.W. and Foehrenbach, L.M. (1991) 'The addiction to negativity.' *Psychoanalytic Review 78,* 3, 391–410.

Laub, D. and Auerhahn, N.C. (1993) 'Knowing and not knowing: Massive psychic trauma: Forms of traumatic memory.' *International Journal of Psycho-Analysis 74,* 287–302.

Lewis, H.B. (1981) 'Shame and guilt in human nature.' In S. Tuttman, C. Kaye and M. Zimmerman (eds) *Object and Self: A Developmental Approach: Essays in Honor of Edith Jacobson.* New York: International Universities Press.

Loftus, E. (1996) 'Memory distortion and false memory creation.' *Bulletin of the American Academy of Psychiatry and the Law 24,* 3, 281–295.

Loftus, E. (1997) 'Creating false memories.' *Scientific American 277,* 3, 71–75.

Maltsberger, J.T. (1993) 'A career plundered.' *Suicide and Life-Threatening Behavior 23,* 4, 285–291.

Martin, J. (1997) 'The season of sharing grief.' *Washington Post,* 5 January.

Masterson, J.F. (1977) 'Primary anorexia nervosa in the borderline adolescent: An object relations view.' In *Borderline Personality Disorders: The Concept, The Syndrome, The Patient.* P. Hortocollis (ed) New York: International Universities Press.

McGuire, J. (1997) 'Psychosocial approaches to the understanding and reduction of violence in young people.' In *Violence in Children and Adolescents,* V. Varma (ed) Bristol, PA: Jessica Kingsley Publishers, Ltd. (pp.65–83).

McHugh, P. (1995) 'Resolved: Multiple personality disorder is an individually and socially created artifact. Affirmative.' *Journal of the American Academy of Child and Adolescent Psychiatry 34,* 7, 957–959.

McLaughlin, J.T. (1961) 'The analyst and the Hippocratic Oath.' *Journal of the American Psychoanalytic Association 9,* 106–123.

McLaughlin, J.T. (1995) 'Touching limits in the analytic dyad.' *Psychoanalytic Quarterly 64,* 433–465.

Melville, H. (1949) *Moby Dick.* New York: The Literary Guild of America, Inc.

Melville, H. (1961) *Billy Budd and Other Tales.* New York: The New American Library.

Merskey, H. (1996) 'Ethical issues in the search for repressed memories.' *American Journal of Psychotherapy 50,* 3, 323–335.

Miller, A. (1994) *The Drama of the Gifted Child.* New York: Basic Books. First published 1981.

Miller, R.K., Maier, G.J., Van Rybroek, G.J. and Weidemann, J.A. (1989) 'Treating patients "doing time": A forensic perspective.' *Hospital and Community Psychiatry 40*, 9, 960–962.

Mitscherlich-Nielsen, M. (1989) 'The inability to mourn today.' In D.R. Dietrich and P.C. Shabad (eds) *The Problem of Loss and Mourning: Psychoanalytic Perspectives.* Madison, CT: International Universities Press.

Moldawsky, S. (1997) 'Managed care and psychotherapy are incompatible.' *APA Monitor,* July.

Niederland, W.G. (1968) 'Schreber and Fleschig: A further contribution to "the kernel of truth" in Schreber's delusional system.' *Journal of the American Psychoanalytic Association 15*, 4, 740–748.

Niederland, W.G. (1974) *The Schreber Case: Psychoanalytic Profile of a Paranoid Personality.* New York: Quadrangle/The New York Times Book Co.

O'Brien, K.P. (1998) 'Pivotal issues in forensic psychiatry.' *Australian and New Zealand Journal of Psychiatry 28*, 354–357.

Olinick, S.L. (1964) 'The negative therapeutic reaction.' *International Journal of Psychoanalysis 45*, 540–548.

Olinick, S.L. (1978) 'The negative therapeutic reaction: A retrospective fifteen years later.' *Journal of the Philadelphia Association of Psychoanalysis 5*, 165–176.

Palm, K.M. and Gibson, P. (1998) 'Recovered memories of childhood sexual abuse: clinicians' practices and beliefs.' *Professional Psychology: Research and Practice 29*, 3, 257–261.

Parens, H. (1979) *The Development of Aggression in Early Childhood; Coping with it Constructively.* New York: Jason Aronson Inc.

Parens, H. (1991) 'A view of the development of hostility in early life.' *Journal of the American Psychoanalytic Association 19*, 75–108.

Parens, H. (1998) *The Roots of Prejudice.* (unpublished).

Paris, J. and Frank, H. (1983) 'Psychological determinants of a medical career.' *Canadian Journal of Psychiatry 28*, 354–357.

Parker, H. (1996) *Herman Melville, A Biography.* Vol. 1, 1819–1851. Johns Hopkins University Press.

Pattison, E.M. (1965) 'On the failure to forgive or to be forgiven.' *American Journal of Psychotherapy 19*, 106–115.

Phillips, J. (1996) *The Magic Daughter: A Memoir of Living with Multiple Personality Disorder.* New York: Viking Press.

Pick, I.B. (1995) 'Concern: Spurious or real.' *International Journal of Psychoanalysis 76*, 257–270.

Poland, W.S. (1984) 'On the analyst's neutrality.' *Journal of the American Psychoanalytic Association 32*, 283–299.

Poland, W.S. (1996) *Melting the Darkness: The Dyads and Principles of Clinical Practice.* Northvale, N.J.: Jason Aronson.

Pollock, G.H. (1978) 'On siblings, childhood sibling loss, and creativity.' *Annual of Psychoanalysis 6*, 443–481.

Putnam, F.W. (1995) 'Resolved: Multiple personality disorder is an individually and socially created artifact: Negative.' *Journal of the American Academy of Child and Adolescent Psychiatry 34*, 960–962.

Rank, B. (1949) 'Aggression.' In *The Psychoanalytic Study of the Child.* Vol. III/IV. New York: International Universities Press, pp.43–48.

Richmond, J.B., Eddy, E. and Garrards, S. (1954) 'The syndrome of fecal soiling and megacolon.' *American Journal of Orthopsychiatry 24*, 391–401.

Robertson-Lorant, L. (1996) *Melville: A Biography.* New York: Clarkson Potter Publishers.

Rochlin, G. (1973) *Man's Aggression: The Defense of the Self.* Boston: Gambit.

Roth, H. (1991) *Call it Sleep.* New York: Farrar, Straus and Giroux.

Roth, P. (1969) *Portnoy's Complaint.* New York: Random House.

Russakoff, D. (1998) 'Out of grief comes a legislative force.' *Washington Post,* 15 June, p.A1

Salzman, L. (1973) *The Obsessive Personality.* New York: Jason Aronson, Inc.

Samenow, S. (1984) *Inside the Criminal Mind*. New York: Times Books.

Schetky, D. and Colbach, E. (1982) 'Countertransference on the witness stand: a flight from self?' *Bulletin of the American Academy of Psychiatry and the Law 10*, 115–121.

Schetky, D. and Guyer, M. (1990) 'Civil litigation and the child psychiatrist.' *Journal of the American Academy of Child and Adolescent Psychiatry 29*, 6, 963–968.

Schreber, D.P. (1903) *Denkwurdigkeiten eines Nervenkranken*. Leipzig: Mutze.

Schrut, A. (1964) 'Suicidal adolescents and children.' *Journal of the American Medical Association 188*, 13, 1103–1108.

Searles, H.F. (1965) 'The psychodynamics of vengefulness.' In *Collected Papers on Schizophrenia and Related Subjects*. London: The Hogarth Press.

Seligman, M.E.P. and Levant, R.F. (1998) 'Managed care policies rely on inadequate science.' *Professional Psychology: Research and Practice 29*, 3, 211–212.

Shabad, P.C. (1989) 'Vicissitudes of psychic loss of a physically present parent.' In D.R. Dietrick and P.C. Shabad (eds) *The Problem of Loss and Mourning: Psychoanalytic Perspectives*. Madison, CT: International Universities Press.

Shapiro, W. (1997) 'Mama mia, that's a mea culpa.' *Time*, 30 June, p.18.

Shengold, L. (1994) 'Envy and malignant envy.' *Psychoanalytic Quarterly 63*, 4, 615–640.

Shpancer, N. (1997) 'Displeasure points: Conceptual and logical weakness in Kagan's critique.' *American Psychologist, 52*, 1242–1243.

Schreiber, F.R. (1974) *Sybil*. New York: Warner Books.

Simon, S.B. and Simon, S. (1990) *Forgiveness*. New York: Warner Books, Inc.

Sleek, S. (1998) 'APA guide helps psychological evaluations in child-abuse cases.' *APA Monitor 29*, p.24.

Slevin, P. (1998) 'Faith brings forgiveness in brutal carjacking.' *Washington Post*, 3 April, p.A 20.

Smedes, L.B. (1984) *Forgive and Forget*. San Francisco: Harper and Row.

Socarides, C.W. (1977) 'On vengeance: The desire to "get even".' In C.W. Socarides (ed) *The World of Emotions: Clinical Studies of Affects and their Expression*. New York: International Universities Press.

Spitz, R. (1960) 'Discussion of John Bowlby's paper.' In *The Psychoanalytic Study of the Child*, Vol. 15, pp.85–94. New York: International Universities Press.

Stock, N. (1970) *The Life of Ezra Pound*. New York: Random House.

Strasburger, L.H., Gutheil, T.G. and Brodsky, A. (1997) 'On wearing two hats: Role conflict in serving as both psychotherapist and expert witness.' *American Journal of Psychiatry 154*, 4, 448–456.

Strasburger, L.H., Jorgenson, L. and Sutherland, P. (1992) 'The prevention of psychotherapist sexual misconduct: Avoiding the slippery slope.' *American Journal of Psychotherapy 46*, 4, 544–555.

Strean, H.S. (1979) 'The unanalyzed "positive transference" and the need for reanalysis.' *Psychoanalytic Review 66*, 493–506.

Stromberg, C. and Dellinger, A. (1993) 'Malpractice and other professional liability. The Psychologist's Legal Update.' *National Register of Health Service Providers in Psychology 3*, p.13.

Symington, N. (1996) *The Making of a Psychotherapist*. Madison, CT: International Universities Press.

Thigpen, C.H. and Cleckley, H.M. (1992) *The Three Faces of Eve*. Atlanta, Georgia: Published by the authors.

Thomas, A. and Chess, S. (1977) *Temperament and Development*. New York: Brunner/Mazel

Thomas, A. and Chess, S. (1980) *The Dynamics of Psychological Development*. New York: Brunner/Mazel.

Thomas, A., Chess, S. and Birch, H.G. (1968) *Temperament and Behavior Disorders in Children*. New York: New York University Press.

Ticho, E.A. (1972) 'The nature of the patient's problems and how in psychoanalysis the individual works to solve them.' *Psychoanalytic Forum 4*, 135–172.

Toolan, J.M. (1974) 'Masked depression in children and adolescents.' In S. Lesse (ed) *Masked Depression*. New York: Jason Aronson.

Torrey, E.F. (1984) *The Roots of Treason*. New York: McGraw-Hill Co.

Tsiantis, J., Sandler, A., Anastasopoulos, D. and Martindale, B. (eds) (1996) *Countertransference in Psychoanalytic Psychotherapy with Children and Adolescents*. Madison: CT International Universities Press, Inc.

Turgay, A. (1989) 'An integrative treatment approach to child and adolescent suicidal behaviour.' *Psychiatric Clinics of North America 12*, 4, 971–985.

Tutu, D. (1998) Interview with Colin Greer. 'Without memory, there is no healing. Without forgiveness, there is no future.' *The Washington Post*. Parade Magazines. 11/01/98.

Van Marle, H. (1997) *Challenges in Forensic Psychotherapy*. London: Jessica Kingsley Publishers, Ltd.

Waldinger, R.J. (1993) 'After the Bean-Bayog case: Psychotherapy on trial.' *Harvard Review of Psychiatry 1*, 62–63.

Wallechinsky, D. (1996) 'He killed my child, but I don't want him to die.' *Washington Post, Parade Magazine*, 18 January, 4–5.

Weiss, J. (1990) 'The nature of the patient's problems and how in psychoanalysis the individual works to solve them.' *Psychoanalytic Psychology 7*, 105–113.

Weiss, J.M. (1998) 'Some reflections on countertransference in the treatment of criminals.' *Psychiatry 61*, 2, 172–177.

Welch, B. (1996) 'Suing managed-care companies: the work begins.' *Psychologist- Psychoanalyst 16*, 4.

Welldon, E.V. and Van Velsen, C. (1997) 'Forensic psychotherapy: The practical approach.' In E.V. Welldon and C. Van Velsen (eds) *A Practical Guide to Forensic Psychotherapy*. London: Jessica Kingsley Publishers.

Werman, D.S. (1993) 'E.A. Poe, James Ensor and the psychology of revenge.' *Annual of Psychoanalysis 21*, 301–314.

White, J.E. (1997) 'Sorry isn't good enough.' *Time*, 30 June, p.35.

Wiesenthal, S. (1976) *The Sunflower*. New York: Schocken Books.

Winnicott, D.W. (1958) 'Hate in the countertransference.' In *Through Pediatrics to Psychoanalysis*. London: The Hogarth Press.

Winnicott, D.W. (1963) 'Psychotherapy of character disorders.' In *The Maturational Process and the Facilitating Environment*. New York: International Universities Press.

Winnicott, D.W. (1971) *Playing and Reality*. New York: Tavistock Publications.

Winnicott, D.W. (1975) 'Aggression in relation to emotional development.' In *Through Pediatrics to Psychoanalysis*. London: The Hogarth Press.

Winnicott, D.W. (1984) *Deprivation and Delinquency*. New York: Tavistock Publications.

Wolberg, A.R. (1979) *The Borderline Patient*. New York: Intercontinental Book Corporation.

Wolfenstein, M. (1966) 'How is mourning possible?' In *The Psychoanalytic Study of the Child 21*, 93–123. New York: International Universities Press.

Yarborough, M. (1997) 'The reluctant retained witness: alleged sexual misconduct in the doctor/patient relationship.' *Journal of Medicine and Philosophy 22*, 345–364.

Yardley, J. (1989) 'The fetters of the past.' *Washington Post Book World*, 22 February, p.3.

Yochelson, S. and Samenow, S.E. (1976; 1985; 1986) *The Criminal Personality*, Vols. I, II and III. Northvale, N.J.: Jason Aronson.

Zola, E. (1942) *Germinal*. London: The Nonesuch Press.

Subject Index

Author Index